Money Matters

Harriet Wilson worked for five years for the Consumers' Association and was responsible for financial and other features for the national press and television. During this period she became involved with *Money-Go-Round* researching viewers' queries on budgeting, money problems, etc. Harriet Wilson is also a freelance journalist who has contributed numerous articles to magazines such as *Living* and the *Sunday Times* colour supplement.

Also published by Pan Books

Buy Right
The *Money-Go-Round* guide
to Consumer Affairs

Harriet Wilson

Money Matters

The *Money-Go-Round* guide
to Personal Finance

illustrated by Jim Friell

Pan Books London and Sydney

Whilst the advice and information in this book is believed to be true and accurate at the time of going to press, neither the author, the publisher nor Thames Television can accept any legal responsibility or liability for any errors or omissions that may be made.

First published 1981 by Pan Books Ltd,
Cavaye Place, London SW10 9PG
© Harriet Wilson 1981
ISBN 0 330 26180 0
Set, printed and bound in Great Britain by
Cox & Wyman Ltd, Reading

Contents

Introduction 7
1 It's your money 8
2 Your income, and your tax 19
3 Banking and budgeting 35
4 A roof over your head 50
5 Running your home more cheaply 70
6 Live now, pay later 93
7 Saving and investing 111
8 Insurance 122
9 Social security 141
10 Home maintenance and improvements 168
11 Transport and holidays 177
12 Families and children 194
13 Managing in retirement 214
Useful addresses 223

Introduction

Money is the root of all evil – or at least, to judge by the bags of letters we get at *Money-Go-Round* every week, a lot of it. You ask about social security, tax, insurance, mortgages, fuel bills and all the hundred and one other money matters that we all have to cope with in our daily lives.

The problems I dealt with in five years of research for the programme came in all shapes and sizes, from how to fill in a tax return or choose an investment programme, to how to work off a pile of debts that threatened the family home itself. But behind them all was the same basic question: how to manage your money so as to get the best value out of it. With the cost of living going up every day, there's no easy answer; but the more you know and understand the better you will do. So having a reference book at your elbow can really help you to stretch the money in your purse a bit further and avoid a lot of pitfalls as you go.

What I have tried to do in this book is to give some guidelines to help with all the big money matters that people come across, to show you where you can save money and where you should be very careful unless you have money to throw away. With prices rising all the time some of those quoted in these pages may already have gone up since we went to press; but that just makes it all the more important to follow every bit of advice and to keep watching *Money-Go-Round* for all the latest money facts.

Harriet Wilson, 1980.

1 It's your money

It may seem that as long as you have a regular income big enough to cover your living expenses, you need not worry about budgeting. You may also feel that if your income is *not* regular, or *not* big enough to cover your living expenses, then budgeting won't be much use to you.

In fact neither of these assumptions is true. Unless you have a very great deal of money indeed (in which case you need another book, on how to stay rich), budgeting can make the difference between getting by and getting into debt, or between getting by and getting the car, holiday, or house you have always wanted.

It's your money, that you work hard to earn. However much, or little, of it there is, you owe it to yourself, and your family if you have one, to look after it – which means budgeting.

Budgeting does *not* mean feeling miserable every time it's your turn to buy a round; it is knowing *where* the money comes from, *when* it arrives, *how much* there is, and *where* it goes to. We'll start with a look at your income.

You and your income

Your income is, quite simply, all the money that 'comes in'. It may come from several places – your job, a pension, rent from property you let, social security, the contributions of grown-up children living with you, and so on. Few of us have as big an income as we would like, but there are ways of increasing your income without robbing a bank, and of making more of what you do have.

Making more money

Ways of increasing your income include:

1 Getting a job that pays well and, particularly in times of inflation, gives you the chance to earn tips or commission, which will increase in line with the cost of living – salesmen for example. If you run your own business, of course, your income should, in theory, rise in line with prices.

2 Doing overtime or getting a second job – on Saturdays perhaps.

3 Finding an employer who offers extras like a cheap canteen, free or cheap season ticket loans, discounts in shops, or help with buying a house. Some of these benefits are not taxed, which makes them worth even more if you are a taxpayer.

4 Working as close to home as you can. Travel costs a lot, and is bound to cost more in the future.

5 Making the most of all the tax allowances you can get. Even on PAYE you may be able to pay less tax than you have before if you know how to go about it, and you can certainly avoid paying more than you should.

6 Knowing exactly what your rights are in the unhappy event of being made redundant or dismissed. By law, you should get proper notice and payment if you are made redundant, and if you are unfairly dismissed your side of the story should be heard.

7 Providing for your future income by looking carefully at your firm's pension scheme (preferably before you even accept the job), and making your own arrangement if it seems inadequate (see page 221).

8 Paying your National Insurance contributions. Make sure you know what benefits you could claim – and claim them (see Chapters 9 and 12).

Training for a better job

The most obvious way of getting a bigger income is to get a more highly paid job. If you do not have any particular skills, though, you may have to take whatever job you are offered. The way to a better job is qualifications, which you can get either before or after you start working. If you are still at school, ask your teacher to help you decide what to do, or go and see the local authority careers officer in your area during your last year. If you can't find any work, the Youth Opportunities Programme is there to help you. Until you are nineteen, it gives you the chance to try out different sorts of work and learn some basic skills. You will be paid a tax-free allowance while you are on the programme. Ask for details at your local Job centre or careers office.

If you are over nineteen and your full-time education finished more than two years ago, it is still not too late: the TOPS programme will pay you a living allowance while you learn a new skill. Ask at your local employment office or Jobcentre.

The Job Search and Employment Transfer schemes give money to people who are unemployed or threatened with redundancy; they will help them look for a job and assist them in moving to another area where more jobs are available. Ask at your Jobcentre *before* moving or starting work in a new area. You can get help towards the cost of fares to attend interviews and the expenses of moving house.

While you are training you may not have much money, but in the future you are likely to get a better paid and more secure job.

Women should always try to get some qualification or skill. Never assume you will get married and have a husband to support you for the rest of your life. He may lose his job, get ill or even die; you may need more money than he can earn. If any of these things happened – and they do surprisingly often – you would need to support yourself and maybe your children as well.

Fringe benefits

These are payments in kind or non-cash benefits on which you may pay no tax, or less tax than you would if their real value to you was just added on to your salary. If you are wondering whether or not to take a particular job, find out what fringe benefits, if any, the employer offers. If you are an employer, give fringe benefits where you can – you can give more at less cost to yourself.

Fringe benefits include:

- a really good pension scheme, and sick pay scheme;
- luncheon vouchers – up to 15p a day tax free;
- company cars – your private use of it may not be taxed, but even if it is it still works out cheaper than buying your own;
- house purchase loans – probably the most valuable benefit of all, since even if the rate of interest your employer charges is not particularly low, the money is there when building societies may be short of cash to lend, and the loans are tax free if used entirely for buying or improving your home;
- loans for other things, such as season tickets – may be taxed, if you earn more than £8,500 a year and the loan is for more than £200, but still worthwhile since you might pay a lot more to borrow somewhere else, or not be able to borrow at all.

Redundancy and dismissal

None of us likes to think about being suddenly out of a job, but if it were to happen things would not seem nearly so bad if you knew exactly where you stood both legally and financially.

Periods of notice

Unless you have committed an offence, you cannot be dismissed without proper notice. You must be given at least:

- one week's notice if you have been in the job between four weeks and two years;
- one week's notice for each year you have been in the job, from two to twelve years;
- twelve weeks' notice if you have been in the job for more than twelve years.

So you should never find yourself out on your ear without money to last to the end of the week!

Redundancy payments

1 If you are made redundant, you can choose whether to work out your notice, or have a cash payment instead of notice and leave at once. Choosing the cash may be better because it gives you money while you look for another job.

2 If you have been in a job for more than two years when you are made redundant you are entitled by law to claim compensation. The law lays down the least you can get, but your employer may be more generous, or your contract may give you the right to more. Legally you are entitled to:

- half a week's pay for each year in the job between the ages of eighteen and twenty-one;
- one week's pay likewise between twenty-one and forty;
- one and a half weeks' pay likewise between forty and sixty-five (sixty for women).

The most you are allowed is £3,600, which you would receive if you had been in one firm for twenty years or more, after the age of forty, earning at least £120 a week. If you

12

had worked in a job for eight years, earning £60 a week and were thirty-five, you would get £480 (eight times £60).

Unless your payment is based on your contract, compensation for redundancy is tax free up to £10,000, and maybe more. If you are offered voluntary redundancy, look carefully at how much money you would receive, and how easy it would be to get another job – you might do well to take it.

Claiming redundancy money
Not everyone who loses a job gets redundancy money. For you to be 'redundant', one of the following must happen:

- your employer says you are redundant;
- your employer refuses to renew a fixed term contract when it comes to an end;
- you are laid off or put on short time for four weeks running or for any six weeks in thirteen, and your employers will not take you back into full-time work within four weeks;
- your employer won't pay you, or down-grades your job (but you cannot complain if you are asked to do a job that you don't like if it is as good as your old one).

If you really are redundant, you should follow these rules to ensure you get your compensation:

1 Make your claim within six months, first to your employer, then, if he won't agree, to an industrial tribunal.
2 If you need to go to an industrial tribunal, get form IT1 (and the leaflet ITL1 which explains it) from your Jobcentre or Employment Office.
3 If your claim is complicated there may be a 'hearing', which you and your employer will be expected to attend. This is rather like a court, and you can take a friend, trade union official or lawyer to help you. You can't get legal aid but you can get some free legal advice

under the Green Form scheme (see page 212). If you can sort things out without a hearing, do; your employer will probably have better legal help than you, and costs can be awarded against you. Never go ahead with a hearing until you have had expert advice from someone such as your solicitor or trade union.

If you get another job while you are working out your notice, you can still claim redundancy money, but you may not find it so easy to get.

In most cases employers pay redundancy money without any trouble, and even if there is some argument you may well be able to sort it out without going to a tribunal.

Unfair and wrongful dismissal

If you are dismissed without good reason, or without proper warning, you may be entitled to compensation. Always put your case to your employer first, since he may offer you compensation, and if he doesn't you will be no worse off than you were before.

Unfair dismissal
This means you have been dismissed without good reason. If you have been in the job for a year or more, you may qualify for compensation. First talk to your employer, and if he is uncooperative, put in your claim to the industrial tribunal on form IT1. If it is decided that there was no good reason for dismissing you, you may receive a basic award worked out in the same way as redundancy money, and possibly compensation based on your loss of earnings, future prospects and hurt feelings. You could get up to £6,250 tax free; but remember that your employer will probably have good legal advice. *Never* go to a tribunal without taking advice from a lawyer or Citizens' Advice Bureau (CAB) or trade union.

Illegal dismissal
If you are dismissed because of your race or sex, or because you get married, your employer will have committed an offence. Contact the Commission for Race Relations or the Equal Opportunities Commission. You may get your job back or compensation.

Wrongful dismissal
If your employer doesn't give you the amount of notice stated in your contract, or the proper warnings before dismissing you, you can claim whatever pay you lose as a result. Go to your employer first, and if he refuses to pay, get advice before going to a tribunal.

Being self-employed

Some people find the idea of being their own boss very attractive. Many self-employed people do very well, but it is a risky way of life, and you should think extremely carefully before going ahead. Some of the things you should remember are:

1 Unless you also worked for an employer during the relevant tax year, and paid enough Class 1 National Insurance contributions, you won't get the earnings-related part of the state sickness benefit. The basic rate is only £20·65 a week, plus extras for your dependants.
2 You won't get the earnings-related part of the state retirement pension, and the basic rate is only £27·15 for single people and £43·45 for married couples.
3 You won't get any unemployment benefit if your business fails unless you also worked for an employer during the relevant tax year, and paid enough Class 1 National Insurance contributions.

4 Your tax will be far more complicated, and you should always get the advice of an accountant before you start.

These are just a few of the financial points to consider; there will also be the legal ones to find out about. If you decide to go ahead on your own, it is important that you sort out your financial arrangements right from the start.

Decide how to trade
On your own you will be entirely responsible for all the profits, losses and debts of the business, to the last penny of your personal money.

In a limited company you will share the responsibility with other owners, and each of you will only be responsible up to a certain amount of money. For example, Bill Sweet put £10,000 into a business and the other two owners put in £8,000 each. When the firm got into bad trouble, Bill had to find £10,000 for the creditors whereas his co-owners only had to find £8,000 each. Your accounts will be public and will have to be audited.

In a partnership each partner is entirely responsible: if the business gets into debt each will, if necessary, have to pay out every penny of his personal money.

In a limited partnership some, but not all, of the partners can put a limit on the amount of debt for which they will be personally responsible.

The choice is complicated, and you should talk to a solicitor and an accountant about the pros and cons of each before deciding.

Learn how business accounts work
You will need to keep careful records and accounts so that

you know how your business is going, your income tax can be worked out and the VAT inspector can do his job. You may think you will pay less tax if you don't keep proper records, but the taxman will catch up on you in the end, and you will almost certainly pay more than you would have done if your records had been in order.

Learn how tax works

You will need an accountant to help you, but you should at least understand what sort of things you can claim tax relief for. You can claim relief on many more expenses than you can under PAYE, but the rules are complicated. Working clothes are allowed, but other clothes are not; entertaining foreign clients is allowed, but not British ones, and so on. If you don't claim where you can, you will lose a lot of money.

Get your National Insurance organized

If you work for an employer, he takes your National Insurance contribution out of your pay, but if you are self-employed you have to organize it for yourself. Most self-employed people pay Class 2 contributions, which cost £2.50 a week. You can pay through your bank or the National Giro bank by filling in the form in leaflet NI41 from your local social security office. If you do this you won't have to stamp a card, because your contributions will be recorded centrally by the Department of Health and Social Security. Alternatively you can buy stamps each week at a post office and stick them on your card – which you get from your local social security office.

You can get exemption from paying Class 2 stamps if your net profit is £1,250 or less in 1980/81. To do this, get leaflet NI27A from your social security office, but remember that if you don't pay the stamps you might well get a reduced pension, lower widow's benefit, no sickness benefit, or no maternity benefit.

You will have to pay Class 4 contributions, as well as

Class 2, if your self-employed profit or gain is over £2,650 in 1980/81. These contributions cost 5 per cent of your profit from £2,650 to £8,300 – so the most you might have to pay would be £282·50. The money is collected by the taxman along with your income tax.

If you have missed paying some NI contributions, you can pay Class 3 stamps later on, to improve your benefits. These cost £2·40 each, and you can pay them in the same ways as Class 2 contributions; you will need to read leaflet NI42 and fill in Form CF351. You can also pay Class 3 stamps in a lump sum at the end of the tax year. Class 3 stamps count towards your basic pension, but they do not help towards sickness benefit, or the maternity allowance and remember, you can't pay Class 3 contributions for weeks when you should have paid a Class 1 or Class 2 contribution, only for weeks when you were not liable at all.

Get yourself a private pension
If you are self-employed you won't get the earnings related part of the retirement pension, and the basic £27·15, or £43·45 for couples, is not much to live on. See page 221 for how to make your own arrangements.

Get your own health insurance
You will only get the basic £20·65 state sickness benefit plus increases for your dependants; there will be no employer to help out, and your business could suffer badly without you (see page 135).

2 Your income, and your tax

Managing your income tax

As soon as you get a regular job, your employer will tell the tax office that you are working for him. If you earn more than a certain amount you will have income tax taken off your pay. There is no legal way of avoiding this, but if you understand how your tax is worked out you will at least never pay more tax than you must.

Save-it tip
Never assume that the people in the tax office cannot make mistakes – they're only human; if you pay too much tax, you are entitled to have back the extra you have paid, sometimes plus interest. It may be up to you to spot the mistake, so it is important to understand how the system works. Even if the mistake is to your advantage it is better to tell the tax office. They will catch up on the error later when you may not have the cash to pay it back.

Reading your pay slip

Knowing how to read your pay slip is the first step in checking your tax.

Net pay is the amount you get in your pocket.

Basic pay is the weekly, monthly or annual salary stated in your contract.

PAY ADVICE

Kalamazoo
18205-11½x3

	Week or Month No.	Date		
	Details			
Earnings	A			
	B			
	C			
	D			
	E			
	Gross Pay			
Superannuation				
Gross Pay for Tax Purposes				
Gross Pay to Date for Tax Purposes				
Tax Free Pay				
Taxable Pay to Date				
Tax Due to Date				
Tax Refund				
DNS	Tax			
	* N.I. Contribution (Employee)			
	0			
	1			

Deductions	2		
	3		
	4		
	5		
	6		
	Total Deductions		
Net Pay			
F			
G			
Total Amount Payable			
N.I. Contribution (Employer)			
N.I. Total (Employer & Employee)			
H			
* Contracted-out Contribution included above			

YOUR PAY IS
MADE UP AS
SHOWN ABOVE

Gross pay is 'basic pay' plus any overtime or other extras – which may be shown separately as well.

Tax code is the code that represents the allowances you are entitled to. Everyone is allowed some tax-free pay each year – at the moment single people and married women with their own jobs can have £1,375, and married men £2,145. People over retirement age are allowed £1,820 tax-free income each year (£2,895 for couples) and single parents £1,800. On top of that you can be allowed extra tax-free pay if you have a mortgage or certain other responsibilities that have to be paid for (see page 25, 'Filling in the Form'). Whatever is left over – your net taxable income – is taxed at 30p in the £ on your income up to £11,250 a year. If your net taxable income is over that you will pay tax at higher rates.

The number in your tax code is the total of your tax-free allowance with the last figure knocked off. The letter stands for the type of personal allowance you get: 'L' (lower) is for single people and earning wives; 'H' (higher) is for married men and people bringing up children on their own; 'T' is for people who can't or don't want to fit into either of the other groups. For example, Bill Simple is single and has no allowances other than his personal one, so his tax code is 137L; Fred Organizer has a wife, and pays £1,050 allowable mortgage interest. This gives him allowances totalling £3,195, so his code is 319H, and he will not pay tax on the first £3,195 of his earnings.

If your code is wrong you will pay the wrong amount of tax. The letter is easy to check – you know if you're married or not! The number is harder, particularly if you have lots of allowances. To check it you will have to look at the 'notice of coding' that the taxman sends you. It tells you what allowances you have got, and how your code was worked out. If your notice of coding is right, all you have to do is make sure that the same code is used on your pay slip. If you don't agree with the code you have been given, or don't understand it, ask your tax inspector or at any PAYE inquiry office.

Tax is the amount of tax you have paid in this financial year – which is since last April.

National Insurance is what we all have to pay in order to qualify for social security benefits if we are ill, out of work, and so on. The amount you pay depends on how much you earn.

Company pension (or **Co. pen.**) is the pension scheme run by your firm. Not all firms have one, and you may not belong to it even if yours does.

Total deductions is the total of tax, National Insurance, pension scheme and any extras like repayments on a season ticket loan. They are all added together and taken off your gross pay; your net pay is whatever is left.

Save-it tip
When you get your pay slip:
1 If the tax code doesn't look right, ask the pay clerk about it.
2 Make sure you have been paid for any overtime you have done.
3 Check that the total deductions have been added up correctly, and taken off your gross pay correctly.
4 Last but not least, check that your basic pay is right – mistakes can happen.

There is no legal way of evading income tax.

Paying less tax

Tax evasion means concealing facts, or lying, in order to pay less tax. It is against the law. You will be found out in the end, and then you will not only have to pay all the tax you should have paid, but interest and perhaps penalties as well.

Tax avoidance means arranging your money in such a way that you pay as little tax as possible, while keeping within the rules. It is both legal and sensible.

Getting a tax return

Most people can expect to get a tax return, though possibly not every year. It has two purposes: to get a statement of your income, and to check on the allowances you claim. You must fill it in – otherwise you could be fined or, more likely, you may pay more tax than you should. From what you put on your tax return, the taxman works out your *personal allowances* (you are allowed more tax-free pay, for example, if you are married, blind, bringing up children on your own, or elderly and with a modest income), and your *tax reliefs* (on things like the amount of mortgage interest you pay).

If you are married it will normally be the husband who gets a tax return, which he has to fill in for both of you, but in the year you get married you will still each be responsible for your own tax, and may each get your own tax return.

There are three sorts of tax return, for people with different sorts of income.

Form P1
You will get one of these if, for example, your earnings are quite moderate and your tax affairs quite straightforward. Bill Simple, who earns about average wages, has no other

sort of income and no investments, gets a P1. At the end of the tax year his employer tells the taxman what he earned. You probably won't get a P1 every year, so if your circumstances change (you get married, or take a second job in your spare time, for example), you must write and tell your tax inspector. His address will be on your Notice of Coding, or your employer will know it. If you don't write, you will pay the wrong amount of tax.

Form 11P
If you have a larger than average income, investments or more than one job, you will probably get one of these. You may also get one if you are partly self-employed. It is longer and more complicated than Form P1, so take great care when you fill it in, otherwise you could pay more tax than you should.

Form 11
If you are self-employed you will get this form. You can claim tax relief on a lot more of your expenses than employed people can. If you are self-employed you should have an accountant to make sure that your tax is properly managed – it could make a very big difference.

Tips on filling in a tax return

Put in all your income except tax-free social security benefits (see page 26). Where there is a space for some kind of income or spending that you don't have, write 'none', just to be sure there is no mistake.

Claim all the expenses you can (see page 26).

Make sure you get all the allowances you can (see page 32).

Check your return before you sign it, just to make sure

24

that everything is correct, and that you have included all you should.

Return the form within thirty days of receiving it.

Always keep a note of what you put down in case there is a query later on in the year; and make sure you have your tax inspector's address.

Filling in the form

Start at the beginning and work your way through to the end. You will probably get a P1, so we will go through in the order on that form. On the front, underneath the space for your signature, is a box to put a tick in if you or your wife is over sixty-five. Don't be embarrassed; if you or your wife are elderly and your income is modest you might be entitled to an extra tax allowance. This could be as much as £445 for single people and £750 for married couples, which cuts your tax bill by £113·50 or £225 a year if you pay at the basic rate of 30 per cent – well worth having.

Your earnings

There will be a line through the space for your income from your full-time job – your employer tells the taxman what you earn, so you don't have to. (If you get Form 11P you will have to fill in your earnings yourself – put the figure for 'pay' from the P60 form that your employer will give you each May or June.)

If your wife doesn't tell you what she earns, leave a blank in the space for earnings and write a note explaining why. The taxman will find out her income from her employer, and neither of you will be penalized. If you or your wife have a second job, you fill in the income in the space for 'all other earnings'.

Income: tips and incidental receipts are taxable.

You may get an expense allowance for protective
clothing and a tax allowance for the tools of your trade.

Expenses against earnings – one of the 'incidental receipts'
you may get is an expense allowance. You may not have to
pay tax on it if you spend it all on certain things that you
need for your job, and only use in the job – for example,
protective clothing, a uniform, the cost of running your
car during working hours at your employer's request. If
you have to buy the tools of your trade yourself, your union
may have agreed a tax allowance with the taxman. Ask.

Social security benefits and pensions
Almost all are tax-free at the moment, and you need not fill
them in on your tax return. The tax-free ones are: sickness
benefit, invalidity pension, unemployment benefit, maternity
grant, attendance allowance, family income supplement,
supplementary benefit, industrial injury benefits, death
grant, child benefit, NI retirement pensioners' Christmas
bonus and disablement pensions from the armed forces.

You *do* have to fill in your state retirement pension.

If you started receiving it during the year, say when. You have to fill in the amount you had in the whole year, so if if you receive it each week you will have to multiply by the number of weeks you have been getting it. If your wife has a pension on her own National Insurance contributions, remember to put a tick in the box in order to get an extra tax-free allowance.

Save-it tip
Some married women get a bigger pension by claiming on their husband's contributions; this is quite possible if they only worked for part of their life. Ask at your social security office.

Widows and other benefits – this is the space for the social security benefits on which you *do* pay tax: widow's allowance, widow's pension, widowed mother's allowance, industrial death benefit, child's special allowance, mobility allowance, invalid care allowance, and guardian's allowance (see Chapter 9 'Social security').

Other pensions – this includes any pension from your job and any private pension you have bought for yourself.

All pensions – further details – this is where you put in the amounts you receive each week or month for all the pensions you have given the annual amounts for earlier in the form.

Interest not taxed before receipt
This includes any interest you get from bank accounts, private loans, British Savings Bonds, Defence Bonds, War Loan and National Development Bonds, National and Trustee Savings Bank accounts. You should fill in all you get from any of these, although you won't in fact have to pay tax on some of them – such as the first £70 of interest from an NSB ordinary account. You do not have to fill in

tax-free investments like SAYE, National Savings Certificates and premium bond prizes.

Interest from building societies
This means just what it says. You should fill in whatever you have received even though you only have to pay tax on interest from building society accounts if you pay tax at more than the standard rate of 30 per cent.

Dividends from UK companies and unit trusts
Here you put in any dividends you have had from shares or unit trusts, plus the amount of tax credits. Give the name of the company, the number of shares you own and the amount of the dividend and tax credits. If you are not liable for tax then the taxman owes you the amount of the tax credit, so write and tell him.

Other dividends, interest, etc.
This space is for interest you get from investments in, for example, local authority bonds. Do not put down what you actually received, because tax has already been paid. You should find out how much the interest was *before* tax was taken off – which the local authority concerned can easily tell you if it's not clear from the voucher that came with the interest. If you don't have to pay tax, the taxman owes you money, because the interest you received had already had tax taken off. Write and tell him.

Rents
This includes any income you get from letting furnished or unfurnished property, or land, and includes things like paying-guests in your home or bedsitters in a house you own and run as a business. If there isn't room on the form, write the details on a separate sheet of paper.

Save-it tip
Remember to include all the expenses of letting any property from which you receive income, including:

- rent or rates, if you pay them;
- maintaining and repairing the building;
- insurance;
- cost of providing services (lighting for a hall, or a cleaner perhaps);
- management expenses (your own expenses for visiting the property, arranging lettings etc.);
- fees to letting agencies.

Remember to keep the receipts for all these costs as proof. If you let furnished property and provide meals, heating, lighting, cleaning or any other service, you can claim a deduction for what they cost you. You may not get all you claim – the rules are very complicated and you should talk to your tax inspector.

If your wife runs the letting as her business, you should put the income down as her earnings and claim the extra wife's earned-income allowance.

Profits from trade or business
This space is not for odd jobs (which go further down the form under 'Other income') but for partnerships or businesses. You fill in your profit after taking off expenses, allowances, stock relief and losses.

Other income
If you have any income that is not written down somewhere else, it will go in here.

Alimony and maintenance payments
These are only taxable if paid under a court order or legally binding agreement, so don't put in any payments made

voluntarily. If, under a court order, you get enforceable payments of less than £21 a week (plus £12 a week for each child), or £91 a month (plus £52 a month for each child), just fill in the amount you receive. If you get more than this, tax will have been taken off before the payments reach you, and if you don't have a high enough income to pay tax, you can get it back. Write and tell the taxman.

Any other income
This is the space for income from odd jobs, leaving payments and compensation. You will not normally pay tax on redundancy payments, golden handshakes (unless they top the £10,000 mark), or lump sums awarded for injury.

Your outgoings

Knowing what these are and making the most of them could well save you money.

Interest on loans for purchase or improvement of property
This is just another way of describing the mortgage on your house. If you are borrowing from a building society they will tell the taxman how much interest you pay and there will be a line through this space. If your loan is from anywhere else you will have to get a certificate from the lender to prove how much interest you have paid. Send this certificate in with your tax return.

Save-it tip
You can get tax relief on loans to *improve* your home as well as to buy it, but not to repair it. Things like adding a new garage, or installing full central heating count as 'improvements'. Do as much of your borrowing as you can

for things you can get tax relief on, and save your cash for other things.

If you have to get a bridging loan from your bank when you buy your house, you can get tax relief just as if it was a mortgage – at least for a year or so. Put the details here.

Interest on other loans
If you are over sixty-five and buy an annuity secured on your home, you should put the details here.

Other outgoings
This does *not* mean everything else you spend! If you pay alimony or maintenance, this is the place for the details. You will only get tax relief on regular payments made under a court order or legally binding agreement. So these have the advantage of cutting your tax bill. If the order is for less than £21 a week (plus £12 for each child), or £91 a month (plus £52 for each child), put down what you pay and write 'without deduction of tax'. If you pay more than this, you will have to take the tax off before you pay the money to your wife or ex-wife; for example, the court ordered Jim Separate to pay his ex-wife £95 a month. He has no children so this is over the limit for making the payment without deduction of tax – or 'gross' as it is called. He therefore has to take off tax at the basic rate of 30 per cent from each payment. On his tax return he puts the total £1,140 a year which the court ordered, even though after deducting basic rate tax the amount he actually pays his ex-wife is £798 a year.

If you make voluntary payments to your ex-wife, do not enter them on the form at all.

Capital gains
You may have to pay Capital Gains Tax when you dispose

of something – even if you didn't buy it in the first place, but inherited it, for example, or don't sell it, but give it away. Not many people pay the tax because:

- your capital gains can add up to £3,000 a year before tax has to be paid;
- you don't have to pay tax when disposing of your home, your car, or personal belongings worth less than £2,000 a piece, however big the profit. Don't fill these in on the form;
- you don't pay tax on money from insurance policies, or bonuses on SAYE, National Savings Certificates, Defence Bonds or National Defence Bonds. Do not fill these in on the form.

Allowances

This section of the tax return is where you fill in details of your personal circumstances. It may seem nosy of the taxman to ask for so many personal details, but the object is to see what allowances you are entitled to, and to make sure none are left out. There may be special circumstances that may make your life more expensive, for which an allowance can be claimed that you might not realize you could get.

All you have to do is fill in the names and other details in the spaces provided. It is quite simple, but there are a few points to watch:

1 You can get an extra allowance if you are bringing up children on your own, or with a completely disabled wife.
2 You can only get the blind person's allowance if you are registered as blind. It is worth £54 a year, so it is well worth registering if you can. You don't have to be totally blind – ask your optician.
3 The space marked 'Death and superannuation benefits'

is for the part of a trade union sub. that goes towards a pension, life assurance and funeral expenses. Check with your trade union how much this is.

4 You can claim for a dependent relative even if they don't live with you. What matters is how low their income is and how much you give them.

Keeping a check on your tax

If you fill in your tax return properly, there are only three things that can easily happen to make you pay the wrong amount of tax. These are:

- your outgoings change;
- your income changes;
- you or the taxman makes a mistake.

If your outgoings change (you get married, or your elderly mother becomes dependent on you, for instance), the taxman will allow you more of your income tax-free.

Save-it tip
To make sure you get the extra allowance as soon as possible, don't wait till you get another tax return; write and tell your tax inspector at once. The same thing applies if you take on a new responsibility like a mortgage – write and tell the taxman.

If you get a pay rise, you need not do anything because your employer will automatically start deducting more tax from your pay. If your pay falls, or stops altogether, you will pay less, or even no tax in the future, and you may also be able to get a tax refund. If your pay falls, but doesn't stop altogether, you shouldn't need to do anything – your employer should simply take less tax off your pay or give you a refund. If you find you are still paying the same amount of tax, ask your employer why. If you stop work altogether, send your P45 form, which your employer must give you when you leave, to your tax inspector. Tell him when you stopped working and ask for a rebate.

If the taxman makes a mistake, write and explain exactly what you think is wrong. If you have forgotten to tell him something – that you have married, for example – it is really your fault not his. Don't worry, write and tell him as soon as you remember – you can claim for mistakes up to six years later.

Write and tell the tax inspector as soon as possible
after you're married.

3 Banking and budgeting

Why have a bank account?

If you are paid weekly, or even monthly, in cash, you may feel it is not worth having a bank account. It is true that any savings you may have might earn more interest and be just as safe and easy to get at if you kept them in a building society account (see page 118). It is also true that it can cost you money to use a bank, but bank accounts do have big advantages:

Keeping cash in the house can be a temptation.

1 You need not carry a lot of cash about with you, or keep it in the house where it can be a temptation to you, as well as to others (see over, 'Current accounts').
2 The bank can help you to spread the burden of your big bills evenly through the year (see 'Budget accounts' page 41).

3 The bank can be a comparatively cheap place to go for a loan, and may allow you to have a credit card which *can* mean absolutely free credit (see Chapter 6).

4 The bank manager can give you valuable financial advice, sometimes for nothing.

In spite of all these advantages, not everyone does need a bank account, and different people need different sorts of account, depending on what they want to use them for.

Do you need a current account?

Current accounts are by far the commonest sort of bank account. Just over half the adult population has one. Are all the rest making a big mistake?

Bill Simple probably doesn't need a current account: he gets paid in cash every Friday, he puts money in the meter for all his gas and electricity, he pays his rent in cash each week, and he always uses cash for his shopping. If you are like Bill, you probably don't need a current account either.

If you are not like Bill, a current account would probably help you. Don't be put off by anything people may say about it being difficult to open one. The High Street banks, including the National Girobank run from post offices, and the Trustee Savings Bank, are all waiting for people like you to walk in and open an account.

You *don't* need to make an appointment.

You *don't* need to have lots of money.

You *don't* need to produce your birth certificate.

You *don't* have to be twenty-one – only sixteen (or younger in special circumstances).

All you *do* have to do is:

Walk in and ask to open an account.

Usually, name two referees – people who have known you for some time (your employer would do fine).

Hand over a pound or two to start off the account.

How to use a current account

The bank will give you: a cheque book, for paying bills and getting out cash for yourself, and a paying-in book, for paying cash and cheques into your account.

It is important to keep both these safe. If you lose your cheque book, tell the bank and police at once, before anyone has a chance to try and take money out of your account.

It is also important to fill in your cheques and paying-in slips properly:

- make sure the date is right;
- make sure you have the correct name of the person you are paying, or they won't be able to put the money into their account;
- write the

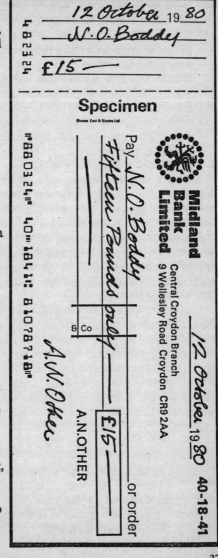

amount of money clearly, in words and figures so there can't be any mistake, and do not leave any gaps where the amount could be changed;

- always sign your name in the same way;
- fill in the stubs as well as the cheques so that you know exactly what you've paid out of your account, and to whom (it is also a good idea to keep a running total of what is left, then there will be less chance of spending more than you've got);
- never, ever, sign a cheque and leave the rest blank. If you do, anyone who gets hold of it can pay themselves whatever they like.

Your bank will also send you a statement, probably each month. This tells you how much money has gone into and out of your account, but, except with the National Giro-bank and a few smaller banks, it won't always tell you who the money has been paid to, or who it came from. If you have written out all your cheque stubs and paying-in slips properly you will be able to go through your statement to make sure it's right. Banks can make mistakes, so always check your statement.

If you pay someone a cheque and then want to halt payment – a shop perhaps, that has sold you faulty goods – you can 'stop' the cheque if you're quick. Telephone the bank at once and tell them the cheque number, the date, the amount, and who it was made out to. You must know all the details (that's another good reason for keeping your cheque stubs properly), and you should confirm what you have said in writing.

Getting cash out of your account

The simple way is to go into your own branch and write out a cheque to yourself; but what if it's out of hours? Or if the queue is so long you can't wait?

Cheque guarantee cards

If your bank will give you one of these you can use it to get up to £50 from any branch of any bank. Also some shopkeepers may cash you a cheque if you have a guarantee card. As long as you are responsible with your money, the bank will probably let you have a card. Remember to keep it very safely; if anyone gets hold of it and your cheque book, they can write out guaranteed cheques.

Cash cards

With one of these you can get money from the 'magic slot machines' outside your bank. Not all banks have them, so if you think you might often need to get cash outside normal banking hours (9.30 a.m. to 3.30 p.m. Monday to Friday) ask about cash cards before you choose your bank.

The National Girobank

Since it is a part of the Post Office, the National Girobank is open during normal shopping hours, including Saturday morning.

Making the most of your current account

There are several easy things you should do to get the best possible value out of your current account:

1 Ask how your bank works out its charges. Most will not charge you anything as long as you keep at least £50 or £100 in your account, but the rules vary a bit from one bank to another. Knowing your bank's rules could save you quite a few pounds a year.

2 Ask your employer to pay your wages straight into your bank account. That way your bank manager will know that money comes in regularly and should be happier

to give you a cheque guarantee card, a credit card or a loan.

3 Arrange for all your regular bills like your rent or mortgage, HP, telephone rental, insurance, and so on, to be paid by 'standing order'. This means that you tell your bank to pay a certain sum of money to a certain person or company at regular intervals, until you inform them otherwise. Then you can be sure that all those bills will be paid on time.

4 Use the 'bank giro' slip that often comes with a bill. Fill it in and hand it to the bank cashier with your cheque, and you can save the postage. If you have several bills to pay at once by bank giro, you can add them up and use one cheque for the lot. You will have to go to your own branch to do this, but you may save bank charges as well as postage.

Remember

You can pay cash, cheques, money and postal orders into your bank account just by walking into any bank; it need not be your own.

You can pay money into anyone else's account, wherever they live, so long as you know their bank, branch and account number – no more worries about sending postal orders.

You should *never* sign a cheque and leave the rest blank – you never know who might get hold of it.

You can't stop a cheque if you use your cheque guarantee card, so be careful what you use it for.

Bank accounts for couples

Any bank will let a husband and wife have a joint current account.

You will each be given a cheque book, so it is important to keep a very careful record of what each of you spend, and compare notes every week or so. Always decide exactly what gets paid for out of the joint account and what, if anything, you each pay for out of your own pockets. Some couples decide they will only have a joint account, but this may not be the best idea; a joint account is very useful for the family budget, but it's important to have a bit of money to do what you like with as well.

Budget accounts

You can have a budget account at most of the High Street banks, including the National Girobank. They are a great help in spreading the burden of the big bills, and making sure that the money is always there to pay them.

You add up how much all your big bills (gas, electricity, insurance, car tax, rent, holiday, and so on) are likely to be over the next year. Divide the total by twelve to tell you the average for each month. Then you pay that amount into your budget account each month, and pay the bills whenever they arrive. If several come at once, the bank will let you overspend because it knows that over the whole year your balance will even out again.

Bill Organizer has a budget account, it works like this:

fuel bills	£200	paid quarterly
season ticket	£100	paid annually
rates	£200	paid annually
telephone	£ 80	paid quarterly
TV licence	£ 30	paid annually
car insurance	£ 50	paid annually
car tax	£ 60	paid annually
house insurance	£ 50	paid annually
saving for holiday	£100	paid annually
TOTAL	£870	

Bill pays £72·50 into his budget account each month (£870 divided by twelve) to cover all those bills. His bank charges him £10 a year for running his account, but he thinks it is worth it because:

– he doesn't have to worry that the rates, gas bill and car tax will all need to be paid at the same time;

– he saves money by getting an annual season ticket (see page 182), and paying his insurance premiums once a year;

– he has standing orders from his current account to his budget account, and from his budget account to his insurance company and the electricity board – that way he can leave most of the worries to the bank's computer and get on with his holiday knowing the money will be there to pay for it.

Leave your worries to the bank's computer and get on with your holiday.

Deposit accounts and savings accounts

These are places to put money you are saving. You can't get the money out just by writing a cheque, but the bank does pay you interest. If you want to decide on the best place for your savings, see Chapter 8.

Spending or budgeting

When the Chancellor of the Exchequer presents his budget we are all probably most interested in how much he will put on a pint of beer or a gallon of petrol, how much he'll raise or lower income tax, or what he'll do about the old age pension. These individual changes are carefully designed so that when they are added together there is enough money to pay for all that the government spends on schools, roads, defence, hospitals, aid to industry – and the civil servants to organize things.

Since there is never so much money that the Chancellor can spend as much as we'd all like on hospitals *and* schools *and* old age pensions *and* aids to industry, he has to decide how to divide up the total 'cake' to give as much benefit as possible to all the things that need money. So one of the most important parts of budgeting, yours or the Chancellor's, is to decide on an order of priorities; more to hospitals means less to something else; more of your budget on a new car means less on something else.

You and your budget

You may say, 'But my money isn't that complicated. I simply get paid on a Friday and spend the money on what I need till next Friday.' You can manage like that, but if you do, ask yourself a few questions:

1 If something unexpected happens – you or one of your children decides to get married, your car collapses, or your child's new school demands a brand new uniform – will you have enough spare cash to pay the bill?
2 When the big bills like electricity or car tax arrive, do you always have the money ready to pay them?
3 Do you know how much you spent on food or petrol last week? If not, you can't possibly tell whether you're being extravagant or wasteful in one direction, while

forced to give up something else – which you might have rather had.

4 If you're lucky enough to have anything left over at the end of the week, are you certain you're making the most you can out of it? Are you putting it into the savings scheme that will give you the biggest profit, or does it sit in a jar on the mantelpiece?

5 Have you ever had to borrow just a bit more than you could really afford, without knowing quite how the need crept up on you? If so, you've been quite a way down the road to bad debt.

If you are not absolutely happy about your answers to all those questions, then it's time you started budgeting. Then you will be able to be certain exactly how much money you have got, and you will know that you are spending it in exactly the way you really want to.

How to start budgeting

Even if you agree that budgeting sounds like a good idea, you may think it will take a lot of time and be boring. Not true. Budgeting can even be fun (especially when you begin to see the results), and with a bit of organization it certainly need not take long.

You will need an exercise book to keep your weekly or monthly accounts in, and a little notebook to carry round with you so that you can jot down what you spend as you go along. If you try to remember what you've spent at the end of a week, or even a day, you will soon see how badly you need a budget!

Your budget will have three sections:

1 Your income from all sources, including earnings, social security, and so on.
2 Your fixed expenses like rent, rates, fuel bills, etc.

3 Your everyday expenses like food, entertainment, fares, etc. You will need to keep a record of all these every month, which is easy if you write them out like this:

	JAN.	FEB.	MARCH	APRIL	(etc.)

Income
wages
wife's
son's
TOTAL

Fixed expenses
rent
rates
electricity
HP for TV
road tax
insurance
TOTAL

Everyday expenses
food
clothing
transport
entertainment
cleaning
TOTAL

You will need to have headings to suit your particular circumstances, but something along these lines will be right for everyone.

Your income
Here you should write down all the income which you are absolutely certain of getting. This will be things like:

- your basic take-home pay, and that of your husband or wife, plus any definitely regular overtime;
- social security benefits or pensions;
- money that your children contribute regularly;
- rents from property you let;
- any other regular income or definite profit or gift you will be getting;
- remember: write down only money you are certain of;
- if your income is irregular (if you are self-employed, perhaps), average your income out over twelve months;
- always put down your actual take home pay, *after* taking off tax, National Insurance, and so on;
- if you aren't sure how much you'll get, put down the minimum;
- if you aren't sure you'll get the money, don't write it down at all.

Your fixed expenses

Here you should write down all the big regular bills, like rent or mortgage, rates, electricity and gas, telephone, HP instalments, insurance premiums, car tax, and so on.

If you find that these add up to more than your income, then you are going to have to change your ways, either to cut down the expenses or to increase your income. Your problem is more likely to be that while your *total* income over the whole year is big enough for your needs, if two big bills come in at once you find it hard to cope. A bit of reorganization should soon put this right:

- a budget account at the bank would spread the burden of all the bills evenly over the year (see page 41);
- you can pay the rates in ten instalments each year – ask the local authority;
- you can spread the cost of gas and electricity with one of the Boards' payment schemes (see page 76);
- you can ask your landlord, insurance company, etc., if you could change the dates of your instalments so that they don't come at the same time as each other;

- remember: write down all the things you *have* to pay for when the bill comes through the door;
- put down the most that you are likely to have to pay. The idea is to see how much money you need to live as you do now, and if there isn't enough, then you will have to start cutting back; you'll never get things straight if you cheat and underestimate how much you are spending at the moment;
- if you put money in a regular savings scheme, write the amount for each month in this section of your budget. (Savings may not feel like a fixed expense because the money is still yours – but if you really want to save, then you don't want to dip into the float you build up, so you should think of it as being just as 'fixed' as the rent.)

Your everyday expenses
Now that you know exactly what your income is, and how much of it you need for the big bills, you can easily see how much is left over for everyday expenses. You may be able to economize on some of these, but there will be a minimum which you simply must have for food, clothes, cleaning and all the other things we all need.

To get a good idea of how much you are spending on these at the moment, write down absolutely everything you spend every day for a month. This is easiest if you divide your spending into categories and days:

	Mon	Tues	Wed	Thur	Fri	Sat	Sun
Food							
Drink							
Tobacco							
Transport							
Entertainment							
Clothes							
Household cleaning, etc.							
Children's extras							

Everybody will have a slightly different list of headings; some may spend money on the garden, others may not drink or smoke. Decide your own categories to suit your own spending pattern.

After a month you should have a clear picture of how much you spend, on what. You may be surprised at how much goes on things you never thought you spent a lot on; perhaps you will want to cut down. You will also see where you really can't spend any less. You may realize that while your total spending is not too high, you are spending more than you'd like to on one sort of thing, and less on another. Now that you know where the money goes it will be much easier to see how to spend less – if you need to – and to make sure that you spend your money in the ways you really want to.

Looking ahead

Careful budgeting won't only help you to have enough money, going where you really want it to go, it will also enable you to be ready for the unexpected. It is always a good idea to have a month or two's income set aside for an emergency – happy or unhappy. It need not be wasted; if you put it in a good savings scheme it will earn interest for you.

If you are planning for a holiday, a new house, a baby or any other future expense, then a careful budget will tell you how much you can set aside each week to pay for it. And if you are short of money, your budget will help you to see where you might economize a bit in order to be able to save.

Final points to remember

1 If you're married, always draw up a joint budget. Otherwise things will get impossibly complicated – and probably lead to arguments.

2 Again if you are married, always allow yourselves some personal money to do what you like with. It may not be possible to have much, but things can get pretty miserable if you can't buy a pint of beer or a pair of tights without telling your partner. Try to be realistic about how much you each need – if one of you has fares to pay and the other doesn't, then that person will need a bigger allowance. Your personal allowances should be written down as a fixed expense.

3 Always allow yourselves a few luxuries; the fewer you can afford the more important it is to notice when you have them.

4 If you are really overspending, rather than just being badly organized, then you must work out a plan to get back on to an even keel, and stick to it. Be realistic. Don't imagine that you can cut your food bill by half, give up smoking and start walking to work all at the same time – or at all. Think instead about the big expenses: do you really need a big car? Could you cut down your fuel bills (see page 71)? Should you be buying a colour television at this moment? Think hard about whether you could increase your income too (see page 9).

5 Don't stop keeping records as soon as you think your budget is organized. Life changes all the time – your income goes up, the rates go up, you start a family, you buy a house. All these things change your financial position. So keep your income and expenditure records going month by month, and even if all your money worries don't disappear overnight, at least you will stand the best possible chance of solving them.

4 A roof over your head

We all need a roof over our heads; for the average family rent or mortgage payments take a big bite out of their income and if you have a big mortgage it may take as much as a quarter. Sadly most of us can't afford to live exactly where we would like to, in just the house we would most like to have; but you may be able to get nearer to your dreams than you thought.

Choosing your home

The first step towards finding your perfect home is to think hard about what sort of home you really want. Some of the important things to think about are listed below.

Place
If you have a job you want to stick with, it will save you time and money to live as near to it as you can. Housing may not be that much cheaper out of town, so it is worth comparing the extra cost of travel – to shops and friends as well as to work – with any saving you may make on the house.

Neighbourhood
House prices go up faster in some places than others, and since buying a house is the biggest investment you are ever likely to make, it is important not to buy one in an area that is falling behind. Make sure that new roads or housing

estates aren't planned to be built near by where they might reduce the value of your house.

Shops
About 30p in every pound we spend goes on food, but you can save a lot by shopping around. A good shopping centre makes this much easier, and if you don't want to spend a fortune on petrol it needs to be close by. If you have a big and hungry family this could really make a difference.

Garden
Growing your own vegetables could save you quite a worth-while sum. If you would use a garden, get one.

Are you likely to need more room in a couple of years?

Size
Moving costs a lot of money. The less often you do it the better. If you are likely to need more room in a couple of years, try to get a bigger house now, especially if you are buying rather than renting.

State of repair

You can sometimes get a bargain if you are prepared to take on a place that needs a lot of repairs. If you can do them yourself you could end up with a house worth a lot more than you paid for it (see Chapter 10, 'Home improvements'). But if you're renting, be careful not to put in a lot of work only to find the landlord puts up the rent (see below, 'Is the rent fair?').

Renting a home

Renting a home is not so permanent as buying, but all the same there are some important things to check before signing on the dotted line:

- is the rent fair?
- are you certain you can afford it?
- who is responsible for repairs and decoration?
- who is responsible for the insurance?

Is the rent fair?

The rents of all but the most expensive houses and flats are controlled by the Rent Act – which means that if the rent seems far too high, or if the landlord raises it by a large amount, you can appeal to the Rent Tribunal to have it lowered. It is against the law for the landlord to turn you out or threaten you in any way if you do this, so if you think you have a case, go ahead. The address should be in the phone book under 'Rent Tribunal' or 'Rent Assessment', but if you need help go to your CAB.

Can you afford the rent?

If your rent is high compared with your income and the number of people you have to support, you may be able to get a *rent rebate*. For example, if your income is £70 a week, you have two children, and your rent is £10 a week, you might get a rebate of £3·03 a week. If you have no children and an income of £40 a week, you could get a rebate of £1·43 on a rent of £6. Your *total income* includes any regular overtime, pensions, unemployment or sickness benefit and Family Income Supplement, before tax or National Insurance contributions are deducted. Your *rent* is what you pay *apart* from rates, heating, lighting or water rates; so if your rent includes any of these you should find out exactly how much your actual rent is before applying for a rebate.

You can get a rebate whether your home is furnished or unfurnished, and whether you rent it from the council or a private landlord. If you receive Supplementary Benefit your rent will already be included in what you get, so you can't get a rebate as well!

Ask about rent rebates at your town hall. (Your landlord need never know.)

Can you afford the rates?
If you haven't much money left for paying the rates, you may be able to get a rate rebate. For example, if you have two children, and your income is £70 a week, you could get £1·27 towards rates of £2 a week. If you have no children and your income is £40 a week, you could get £3·34 towards rates of £4. You are not entitled to a rate rebate if you get Supplementary Benefit, because your rates will already be included in what you get.

Save-it tip
You may be paying rates in with your rent without even realizing. Ask your landlord, and if you are paying rates and find it hard to make ends meet, go to the town hall and ask about a rate rebate.

Who has to do the repairs?

Normally tenants do not have to repair the outside of the house, or cope with plumbing, electricity or gas, unless they have a lease for more than seven years. It is always a good idea to make sure about this *before* you move in, otherwise you could get a nasty shock.

Who pays the insurance?

Accidents do happen (see Chapter 8), and it is very important to be insured, whether you rent or own your home. Normally your landlord will insure the building itself, so if there's a fire or a flood for example, he'll get the money to pay for the repair; but you will have to take out insurance for your own belongings (see Chapter 8).

Save-it tip

Water pipes and central heating fittings count as part of the building; so if your carpet is ruined by a burst water pipe you should ask your landlord to claim on his insurance.

Can you be turned out?

As long as you pay the rent, don't damage the property and don't annoy the neighbours, your landlord can't turn you out unless he wants to live in the house himself, or provides some kind of service such as meals.

If you don't pay the rent you can be thrown out, and in the end your belongings can be taken away from you to pay the debt, but there will be quite a long time for you to find the money or get help before this happens.

What to do if you are unable to pay

If you find it hard to pay the rent, the first thing is to make sure you are getting all the social security benefits you can (see Chapter 9) and to ask about rent and rate rebates. If you still can't find the money, don't panic. Your landlord will have to go to a court for permission to take your property. He is not allowed to take any loose money, clothes, bedding worth less than £50 nor any of the tools of your trade and essentials you need for daily life. He can either keep your remaining things till you pay up, or sell them, in which case he must give you any money he makes over and above what you owe him.

If there still isn't enough money to repay the debt your landlord must write and warn you that he is terminating your lease. Then he has to go to court again, and it will decide whether or not you should be turned out. The court will try to do what is best for you as well as fair to your landlord.

Remember: if you can't pay the rent, go to your CAB, Consumer Advice Centre (CAC) or Social Security office. *Don't* borrow money from expensive places (see Chapter 6, 'Credit').

Council housing

Whether or not you can get a local council flat or house to rent will depend on how badly you need one, how many people in the area need one more badly, and how many there are to go round. To give yourself the best chance you should get on the council's list as soon as you can, and make sure the Housing Department knows all the details about your family that might give you extra points. Don't be shy of telling them if you have had any illnesses in the family that are made worse by bad housing, or if your situation changes at all (your elderly mother comes to live with you, or you have a baby, for example).

If you are offered a council house or flat check who is responsible for repairs and insurance, and whether there are any special points in the lease that you should know about (for example, can you keep pets if you want to?).

Remember: As a council tenant you can get rent and rate rebates in just the same way as private tenants.

Buying a house

Owning your own home will not only give you a nice *feeling* of security but it is also probably the best investment you can make. It will cost a lot – perhaps a quarter of your earnings at first – but there are many benefits:

1 Between 1956 and 1978 house prices rose on average by 9·5 per cent a year, while retail prices only rose by an average of 6·9 per cent a year: on average, those who owned a house had an inflation-proof investment.
2 Once the family grows up you can sell the house, buy a smaller one and still have a nest egg left over to retire on.
3 You will get tax relief on your mortgage, which makes it the cheapest sort of loan there is and it cuts your tax bill.
4 During inflation the value of money falls, so the £15,000 you borrow today will be worth very much less in ten years' time. In fact by spreading the repayment of your debt over the 25-year life of the average mortgage, you are actually making inflation work to your advantage!
5 It may take a while, but in the end you will own your own home; whereas if you pay rent you will have nothing to show for it at all.

Even so, it is not always a good idea to buy a house. Before you make the big decision ask yourself:

1 Can I really afford it? Remember the fuel bills, rates, repairs and so on, as well as the mortgage itself. Remember too that you will have to pay solicitors, surveyors, stamp duty, Land Registry fees and the cost of the removal itself, as well as new curtains and a host of other new fittings – all on top of the price of the house itself.
2 Is it the right size? With all those costs of moving you won't want to move again in a hurry.

3 Is the value likely to rise above or below the average? You may be able to tell an area that is 'going up' by the way the neighbours look after their houses – if they are all being smartened up you could be on to a winner. If you are not using a solicitor, or want to find out before you get that far with a purchase, ask at the town hall about plans for any new developments near by; a new road or shopping centre could be an advantage – but not if it is right outside the front door.

Borrowing to buy a house

A loan to buy a house is called a mortgage. Almost all mortgages are from building societies, most are paid back over twenty-five years, and almost everyone with a mortgage gets tax relief on the interest they pay. You won't get tax relief to buy a second house – the country hideaway – nor for loans of over £25,000; but the average mortgage is around £12,000, and most of us can't afford to run two houses at once!

There are various sorts of mortgage, designed to suit everyone's needs. The main ones are:

- repayment mortgages;
- option mortgages;
- endowment mortgages (with or without profits, or low cost).

You could lose money by not choosing the right one. The building society will help you decide which will suit you best, but you should know a bit about the differences.

Repayment mortgages
These are the commonest sort of mortgage. You pay the loan back in monthly instalments over a number of years – normally twenty-five. Each instalment is partly interest on

the debt that still has to be paid off, and partly repayment of the debt itself.

You receive tax relief on the interest part of each instalment, which makes the loan much cheaper. For example, if the interest rate is 15 per cent and you pay the standard 30 per cent rate of income tax, the interest on a £10,000 mortgage will be £1,500 before tax relief but only £1,050 after it. Since the debt is biggest at the beginning, you pay most interest at the beginning, which means you get most tax relief at the beginning. In fact, even after adding on your repayment of the debt itself, your monthly instalments will go up from say £91·50 to £107 over the twenty-five years – but in twenty-five years' time that £107 won't hurt nearly as much as it would now, because the value of money will have fallen. One of the big advantages of repayment mortgages is that if interest rates rise you may be allowed to pay back your loan over a longer period rather than have to raise your monthly instalments.

If you don't pay tax, tax relief is no help to you; you should get an option mortgage instead.

Option mortgages

These are for people who don't earn enough to pay tax at the basic 30 per cent. You can't benefit fully from tax relief so you are allowed to pay a lower rate of interest (and the government makes up the difference to the building society). The monthly repayments stay the same right through the life of the loan, and for the first ten years or so they will be higher than for a repayment mortgage of the same size. For example, a £10,000 mortgage repaid over twenty-five years with an interest rate of 15 per cent would cost £1,098 in the first year (with tax relief) whereas an option mortgage would cost £1,144·80. But you can comfort yourself with the thought that you will be paying off the debt more quickly – in this case you would pay off £584·55 in five years with the option mortgage but only £323·63 with a repayment mortgage.

You should ask the advice of your building society

58

before deciding which sort of mortgage to go for. If you go for an option mortgage you can't swap to a repayment mortgage for at least four years. If you choose a repayment mortgage you can only change to an option mortgage if your income falls so far that you can no longer claim full tax relief and are actually suffering financial hardship.

Endowment mortgages

Instead of paying back the debt as you go along, you take out a life assurance policy for the same amount as you have borrowed and for the same length of time as your mortgage. Each month you pay the interest on the mortgage loan (but nothing towards the debt itself) and a life assurance premium. At the end of the agreed length of time – probably twenty-five years – the life assurance policy pays out enough to repay your mortgage loan. If you have a 'with profits' policy you will receive two or even three times as much as you owe, so you will have a nice lump sum to spare. Of course, this will cost more than an ordinary repayment mortgage – around 20 per cent more in fact – because you pay a higher interest rate as well as the insurance premium. If you are looking for a good investment over a long period you should look at all the other alternatives before deciding on this one (see Chapter 7), but it has its advantages:

1 Life assurance premiums are treated as if they were paid after tax relief of 17·5 per cent, which could be useful if you pay a lot of tax.
2 If you were to die, the mortgage would be paid off (but you can always make sure of this more cheaply with an ordinary life assurance policy – see page 132).

However, particularly when interest rates are very high, you should look hard at how much an endowment mortgage may cost you.

Low-cost endowment mortgages

These give you the same benefits as an endowment mortgage, and the security of knowing that the mortgage will be paid off if you die, but they cost a lot less than ordinary endowment mortgages. In fact they can cost less than a repayment mortgage. Of course the profit is less than with a full with-profits endowment policy, but you still stand to gain perhaps a quarter as much again as you owe on your mortgage in spare cash at the end of the day. *The big disadvantage of all endowment mortgages* is that if interest rates rise you will have to pay more each month – you won't be given the chance to pay back over a longer period.

The monthly cost of a £10,000 mortgage over twenty-five years at 15 per cent

Repayment	Option	With-profits endowment	Low-cost endowment
15% p.a. £100·50	10·5% p.a. £95·40	15·5% p.a. £90·42 plus £30 insurance	15·5% p.a. £90·42 plus £16 insurance

After twenty-five years you might get £17,500 extra from the with-profits policy, and £2,500 from the low-cost policy. But remember that any profit will be worth a lot less after inflation has taken its toll.

Mortgages for couples

If you are married and are both earning, you can have your incomes added together and get a bigger mortgage (see 'How much can you borrow', page 63). But if one of you is likely to stop working and there will be a family to support, you could find that you have taken on a bit too much. So, never take on a bigger mortgage than you are sure you can manage, and ask if you can pay back more at the beginning in order to pay off as much as you can while there is money to spare.

Escalator and low-start mortgages
With these mortgages you pay less at the beginning and more later on. If you are absolutely certain your income will rise – and can convince the building society – then this could help you. But don't make a decision based on false hopes.

How to get a mortgage

Building societies
More than ninety out of every hundred mortgages are from building societies, and they are the most likely place to get one. However, you will stand a far better chance if:

1 You save with a building society for as long as you can before asking for a mortgage. If you can manage a regular savings scheme, so much the better – it shows you are responsible with money.
2 You choose an ordinary house with nothing that might make it harder to sell.

3 You choose a house or purpose-built self-contained flat, rather than a conversion, or if you do go for a conversion make sure it is sound.
4 You choose a home in good condition – if repairs are needed the building society may not lend you all the money until you have done them.

The local council
Only about two in every hundred mortgages are from local councils, but they do have some advantages:

1 You are more likely to get the whole price of the house – or a bigger proportion of it.
2 You may find it easier to get a mortgage for an older house or a converted flat.
3 Councils may have money to lend when the building societies are very short of funds.
4 They may be more helpful if you haven't got a lot of money.

You will stand the best chance if you have been living in the area for some time. Ask at the town hall, and don't worry if you get sent on to a building society – there is a special arrangement for them to give mortgages to people nominated by the council. Remember to ask about the interest rate, which may be more or less than building societies are charging.

You have a right to a council mortgage if you are buying a council house or flat that you have lived in for at least three years.

Insurance companies
If you want to buy an older property, one that needs a lot of repairs, or you need more than a building society will lend you, it may be worth trying an insurance company. They will insist on linking their loan to an endowment assurance policy, so that they know they will get their money back whatever

happens, and the rate of interest they charge you is also likely to be higher than you pay on your building society mortgage.

All the rest

You can get mortgages from friends, relatives, finance houses, even the person you are buying from. But always be *very* careful about exactly what the terms and conditions of such mortgages are – *never* go ahead without the advice of a solicitor.

How much can you borrow?

This will depend on:

- how much you earn;
- what you have to spend your money on;
- the house you want to buy;
- who you borrow from;
- 'the economic situation'.

Your earnings and commitments

You won't usually be able to get a mortgage at all unless you have a job. If you are self-employed you will have to show audited accounts for the last three years or so to prove that your earnings are what you say they are.

You will probably be able to borrow between two and two-and-a-half times your pre-tax annual earnings – so if you earn £5,000 a year you may be able to borrow up to £12,500. If you are married and both earning, you can have your incomes added together and get a bigger mortgage. Generally you will be allowed up to two-and-a-half times the higher salary plus one times the lower. So if one of you earns £5,000 and the other £4,000, you might get a joint mortgage of £16,500.

It may seem hard when you need a bigger loan than you can get but the limits are set for your own good, so that you don't borrow more than you can afford.

The house you want to buy
Different lenders have different policies about how much they will lend on different sorts of property (see page 61, 'How to get a mortgage'). If the house is old or in bad repair you will almost certainly not be able to borrow much and you may only get a loan on condition that you do the repairs within a certain time.

Even if the house is in good repair and you earn enough to afford it, you probably won't be able to borrow the whole purchase price. The building society, or whoever lends you the money, will have the property valued to see if it is really worth what you are paying for it – they do this because if the worst comes to the worst and you can't pay what you owe them, they will have to sell your house to get their money back. Sometimes they will value a house at less than its purchase price, which probably means they will be willing to lend you less money.

If the building society lends you more than about 80 per cent of the valuation of your new home, you will be asked to take out an insurance policy. You might be asked to take out a policy even on a much smaller loan if the property you are buying is old or not in good repair. This will cost from £70 to £100 or so, but is a once-off payment and may be added on to the building society's loan to you.

Who you borrow from
Building societies do not all have quite the same rules about how much they will lend, so it is always worth finding out the rules of several before deciding which one to ask for a loan. In particular, the rules about adding together the earnings of a husband and wife may be different. On the whole, local councils are prepared to lend a higher proportion of the price than are building societies.

Final tip

If you think you will be wanting a mortgage in a few years' time and know that you will want to buy an older house to do up, or that you and your husband or wife will want a joint mortgage, find out now who will be most likely to lend you the money in those circumstances. If it is a particular building society, you can improve your chances even more by starting to save with that society now.

If you can't borrow enough

Ask yourself whether you are trying to borrow more than you can really afford. Check that you are asking for a loan from the most likely source for the sort of house you are buying. Offer to take out an insurance policy to cover the extra. Ask your bank for a 'topping up' loan.

Remember: it will cost you extra to borrow more than the normal amount. *Never* borrow the extra from people offering 'easy loan' or second mortgages – you could get into bad debt and even lose the house.

The other costs of buying a home

Paying the purchase price is by no means the end of the story. There are a lot of other expenses to buying a house and moving in, and if you don't allow for them from the start you will be in for a nasty shock.

Solicitors' fees

You will have to pay for the building society's solicitor as well as your own – for a £20,000 house you should set aside at least £50 for this. If he acts for you as well he might charge around £200 for your side of the arrangements; if you employ a different solicitor it will almost certainly cost more. It is possible to buy a house without employing a solicitor (although you will still have to pay for the building society's), but you must be absolutely certain you know what you're doing – it will cost even more if you have to get a solicitor to sort out a muddle later on. If the property is old and not registered, things could be complicated, but if the property is registered it will be simpler; if you want to have a go, get a book such as *The Legal Side of Buying a House* (published by the Consumers' Association) and see whether you really understand it.

Surveyors' fees

Again, there could be two men involved, but it will save money to have only one. The building society will employ a surveyor to value the house (and this is all he will do – he will not do a proper structural survey to see if there are any hidden faults like dry rot, and even if he does find something seriously wrong you may not be told). You would have to pay £36 for this building society valuation on a £20,000 house. It is always better to have your own structural survey done too, and with an old house it really is essential. It will be cheaper if you ask the same man to do it while he is at the house doing the building society's valuation, but even so you should allow between £100 and £200.

Land Registry fees

Most property is 'registered' which means that all the details of ownership are recorded at the Land Registry. You have to pay to have the title deeds of your new house sorted out – £50 for a £20,000 house.

Stamp duty

This is just another tax –0·5 per cent of anything you pay for a house over £20,000 rising to 2·0 per cent on houses costing over £35,000. So for a £25,000 house you pay £125.

Removal

This could easily cost over £100, even if you are only moving to a three bedroom 'semi' twenty miles away. Always get estimates from two or three firms; they can vary a lot; better still, hire a van and do it yourself for perhaps a quarter of the price.

The cost of buying a house

Purchase price	Valuation Survey	Land Registry	Building Society's solicitor	Your solicitor	Stamp duty	TOTAL
£12,000	£25	£30	£46	£120	—	£221
£16,000	£32	£40	£50	£160	—	£282
£20,000	£36	£50	£52·40	£200	—	£338·40
£30,000	£46	£74	£58·20	£300	£300	£778·20

Plus VAT on the valuation and all solicitors' fees.

Final tips

1 The price at which a house is advertised is the price the owner hopes to get – but he will always hope for the best, so it is worth offering less. *But* if you do offer less, remember that he may leave his house on the market and accept a higher offer even if he has already accepted yours. This is called 'gazumping', and it can happen at any time before the exchange of contracts – the point at which you pay 10 per cent of the purchase price. The faster your solicitor can get contracts exchanged the less risk there is of being gazumped. In Scotland you can't be gazumped after your offer has been accepted, since a written offer is a binding contract, not made until the purchaser is certain he has the money.

2 You do not have to pay the estate agent – the seller does that. But you will probably have to give him a deposit of £100 or so to show you are serious about buying the house. To be on the safe side you should

only go to members of the Royal Institution of Chartered Surveyors (RICS), the Incorporated Society of Valuers and Auctioneers (ISVA) or the National Association of Estate Agents (NAEA). Members of all these bodies have to keep your money in special accounts, so there is no risk that you could lose it.

3 If you are buying your first home and it is not too expensive, there is a special government scheme to help you. You must save for at least two years in the scheme, which is called the 'Homeloan Scheme' and is run through banks, building societies, trustee savings banks, the National Savings Bank, National Girobank, Ulster Savings and friendly societies. If you have £300 or more in your account for a year you can get a grant of between £40 and £100, depending on how much you saved. If you have at least £600 in your account for a year before you apply you can also get a loan of £600, on which you won't have to pay interest for five years. You have to join the scheme when you start saving, rather than when you buy the house, so if you might be buying a house in the future, join now. It isn't worth putting off buying a house simply to get the grant and loan; by the time you get them, house prices may have risen even more.

What if you can't keep up the payments?

Your mortgage may well be taking a quarter of your income, and if you get ill or are made redundant you may not be able to manage. *Don't panic*, but tell the building society (or other lender) at once. In theory they can sell your house to get their money, but this is *very* unlikely. If you are only going to be short of money for a time – till you get a new job, for instance – they may let you just pay the interest on your loan but no capital for a while. If the difficulty is due to illness, or the death of the breadwinner, you may be able to get help from the social security.

If you can't manage and there is no chance of things improving, try to sell the house yourself rather than have the building society sell it for you. They would charge you for their time and trouble, just when you are trying to spend as little as you can.

Insurance for your mortgage

Very often the reason why people can't keep up with their mortgage payments is that the breadwinner falls ill or dies. For only perhaps £2 a month, so long as you are healthy, you can get an insurance policy that will pay off whatever is left of your mortgage if you should die. For a little bit more you can get cover in case you are ill as well. These policies are cheap and well worth having, so ask your building society or any life assurance company about one.

Selling your house

This is not as expensive as buying, but can still cost quite a bit. Bill Simple's £20,000 house cost him £400 for the estate agent and £180 to the solicitor.

Save-it tip
Try to sell your house yourself rather than through an estate agent. Look around at similar houses to get an idea of price, advertise in the local paper, put up a sign and tell all your friends and neighbours. If you fail, you can always go to an agent later, but a *Which?* survey in May 1979 showed that you stood just as good a chance by going it alone.

You can do the legal side yourself too, but always be very certain you know what you are doing; and remember that when mortgages are hard to get you will have to be patient, as the sale of your house may well depend on a long chain of other sales happening on time.

5 Running your home more cheaply

Whether you own or rent your home, running it will take a very large bite indeed out of your income. Fuel for heat and light will take more than 5p in every pound you earn; food will probably take more than a quarter of your earnings; the machines and furniture you have to make your life more comfortable will probably take another 7p in the pound, and entertainment about the same again. So, keeping warm, fed and comfortable may take half of your entire income – before you have smoked a cigarette, turned on your car engine or been to the cinema. However, there are ways of cutting down these expenses, of obtaining help with the bills or spreading the burden of paying them.

Where to begin

If you have been keeping the record of your spending as described in Chapter 3, you will know how much you spend on fuel, food and drink, entertainment, furnishing and decorating, and so on. All these are things you can probably cut down on, often without lowering your standards at all – quite unlike the rates, mortgage or insurance that you can't do much about, short of moving house! But how?

Look at each of the big areas of expense and divide them into smaller bits. For example, you can divide your fuel bills into heating, lighting, cooking, washing, the freezer and all the other bits of machinery you run. It is much easier to see where you could save if you take each little bit in turn. Some things really are not worth bothering about, others may be costing – or wasting – a small fortune.

Fuel bills

All fuel prices are bound to rise, so you must:
- find ways of using less fuel;
- think twice before buying new machines or central heating – they'll be no good if you can't afford to run them;
- ask about fuel bills in any house you are thinking of buying or renting;
- use the cheapest fuel, and get it at the lowest price.

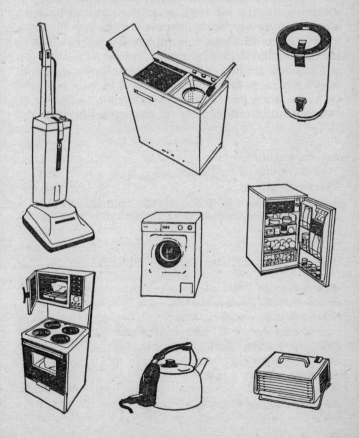

Heating

By far the biggest part of your fuel bill – about 80p in the pound – goes on heating and hot water, so this is the place to start.

Which fuel to use?
If you are moving to a new house, the sort of fuel it needs is an important consideration before you decide to move in. Even if you aren't moving it may, in some cases, be worth changing from one fuel to another; and if you are thinking of installing central heating your choice of fuel could make a difference of hundreds of pounds.

One of the problems with fuel is that nobody really knows which is going to be the cheapest in five, let alone ten years. At the moment the league table for heating and hot water in a well-insulated three-bedroom semi might look like:

	per year
Gas central heating	£213
Anthracite gravity-fed boiler	£259
Oil central heating	£371
Economy 7 electric storage heaters plus top-up heating during the day and an immersion heater	£346

Taking one room on its own you might spend:

Paraffin heater	£58
Smokeless fuel room heater	£65
Gas radiant convector (depending on what other gas appliances you use)	£37-£53
Economy 7 storage heater plus top-up day electricity	£75
Open fire	£87
Bottled gas	£110
Full-rate electricity	£125

Remember that fuel costs vary from region to region, and some areas are colder than others. So always check with local suppliers before you finally decide to get the system that's cheapest to run.

1 Look at how much the different systems cost to install (see below).
2 Think of the practical side – if you have solid fuel you'll have to stoke it every day; if you have gas or oil central heating it must be serviced regularly; if you do not have an outside flue or chimney you can't have solid fuel; if you're out all day and only use a couple of rooms when you come in, warm-air heating will probably be cheaper, and suit your needs better than radiators; if you're out all day storage heaters are a waste since they give out heat continuously, when what you need is a quick burst morning and evening. If you do decide on storage heaters, at least get the sort where you can turn on a boost when you need it.

Buying your heaters
Heaters that are cheap to run may be expensive to buy, so along with knowing what your fuel bills may look like you need to know the purchase prices of the various sorts of heater before you decide which to go for.

For a three-bedroom semi, a central heating and hot water system might cost:

Electricity (4 storage heaters,
  3 panel heaters and 1 immersion)   £840
Smokeless fuel (back boiler and
  6 radiators)   £1,200
Gas (7 radiators)   £1,150
Oil (7 radiators)   £1,300

You can see that although the electric system is expensive to run, it is so much cheaper to install that the overall cost of the electric system would be less in the first year.

The same sort of thing is true with room heaters, the costs for which look something like this:

Electric fan heater	£20
Open fire	£30
Paraffin heater	£65
Gas radiant convector	£105
Electric storage heater	£120
Smokeless fuel room heater	£140

So the smokeless fuel room heater that is quite cheap to run costs so much to buy that it may not be the best bet after all.

When to change fuels
If you have to buy a new heater or heating system to replace the old one, or because there was no central heating before, then you should find out all you can about both purchase and running costs of all the possibilities, and do some careful sums. But more often there already is a heating system; and even if it is one of the more expensive ones to run, you will probably be better off to keep it, because the installation cost of anything else will be more than the saving on running costs. The only times when it is worth scrapping what you've got and starting again are if you use full-rate electricity, or if you use bottled gas for just one room.

Buying fuel at the best price

Whatever fuel you use you will want to pay as little as you can for it.

Solid fuel
Prices can vary a lot, even within one town. Shopping

around could save you up to 20p in the pound – perhaps £50 off your annual bill for a three-bedroom semi.

If you have enough storage space, find a coal merchant who will give you a discount for buying a tonne at a time. Try and find a merchant who will give a discount for payment on delivery – some give as much as 5p in the pound. This would make it well worth saving up for a few months (which makes good budgeting sense too), or using a bank budget account.

Make sure you are using the right sort of solid fuel – a more expensive one may not be right for your boiler. The Solid Fuel Advisory Service has branches all over the country and should be able to sort out any problems of this sort (see address list).

Gas

Prices vary from region to region, but not by anywhere near enough to make it worth moving house!

If you use less than about thirty therms a quarter you will be better off putting money into the meter, but otherwise you should have a credit meter and pay at the end of each quarter (see page 76, 'How to spread the cost of fuel').

If you use more than fifty-two therms a quarter you will pay less for each therm over that amount; so if you already heat by gas, it will pay you to cook by gas too.

If your landlord puts in a gas meter there is a limit to what he can charge for a therm. Ask at your gas showroom.

Oil and paraffin

Prices vary a little with the dealer. Shopping around could save you up to 10p in the pound. Ask about discounts for paying on the nail.

If you have big enough tanks, ask if there is a discount for buying more than say 500 gallons (2,300 litres) at a time – use a budget account to pay the bill.

If you use just a little paraffin for a room heater, go and collect it yourself. You could save a few pence per gallon.

Bottled gas
Prices don't vary much from one brand to another, but whatever sort you use you will pay extra for bottles of less than 10kg.

Electricity
Prices are complicated by the different tariffs. The General Domestic Tariff will be cheapest if you don't use much electricity at night – which you won't if you haven't got storage heaters or an immersion heater. The White Meter, Off-Peak or Economy 7 tariffs will be cheapest for you if you use more than a quarter of your electricity at night. You can check whether you do by reading your meter both at night and in the morning for a week or two. If you have storage heaters or an immersion heater, one of these tariffs will almost certainly be your cheapest bet, but you can get advice from your local showroom on which to choose.

Slot meters always cost more. If your landlord puts one in, there is a limit to what he can charge. Ask in your showroom.

How to spread the cost of fuel

Gas and electricity bills come every three months, but there are several schemes to let you pay as you go along:

1 Buy savings stamps at your local showroom. If you tell them what appliances you use the staff will help you work out how many stamps you need to buy each week; but you don't have to buy the same number each week – just as many as you can afford.
2 Open a monthly budget account at your local showroom. Again, the staff will help you work out how much

you need to pay each month, but with this scheme you must pay your monthly sum regularly. If you sign a standing order for your bank to make the payments, you can forget all about the worry of fuel bills.

3 If you don't want to pay a regular amount each month, or buy stamps, you can open an account at your showroom into which you can pay as much or as little as you like, when you like. It won't be quite so easy to know exactly where you stand, but it may suit your earning pattern better.

Coal and oil suppliers may let you pay your bill in monthly instalments, too, but make sure that you don't pay a lot extra for doing so – a bank budget account might be cheaper, and will help with other bills too.

Getting help with your fuel bills

If you find it hard to pay your bills, don't panic. By insulating and using energy carefully you can almost certainly cut the cost by quite a lot, and if you're really hard up you may be able to get cash help too. Above all, don't just leave the bill unpaid – go to the supplier, explain the problem and you are much less likely to have your supply cut off.

1 If you get supplementary or unemployment benefit, or if everyone in the house is an OAP, go to your social security office for help. If you are over seventy or have small children and are on supplementary benefit, you will get £1·40 a week to help with electricity bills.

2 If you have children under five, or if you get family income supplement, go to the council social services department. Those receiving FIS will get an extra £1 a week for their winter fuel.

3 If you are asking for help in either of these ways, tell the staff at your local showroom; your supply won't be cut off for two weeks – or longer if your case is still being looked into.

4 Whether you get any cash help or not, offer to pay a bit each week to pay off your debt. Decide what you can manage and make sure to pay it every week.
5 If your offer isn't accepted or if you aren't sure you will be able to stick to your payments, ask about having a meter installed, set to pay off your debt as you go along.

How can you use less fuel?

The best way of saving money on your fuel bills is simply to use less fuel. There are lots of ways to save fuel, without living in a cold dark house with only cold food to eat!

Heating
This probably uses half of your fuel, so it is the best place to start saving.

1 Insulate All the heat in a house gets out through the doors, walls, floors, windows, roof and so on in the end, but you can slow the escape down a lot with good insulation. *Draughtproof* all the gaps round doors, windows, skirting and even the letterbox. It shouldn't cost more than £20 for a whole house and could save you twice that in only a year if the draughts were bad. Make sure you leave enough ventilation for gas, paraffin and solid fuel heaters, and remember that although you should certainly block up a grate you don't use, you should put in a ventilation grille. You may be able to get cash for draughtproofing from the social security.

Insulate the loft with at least 80mm (or 100mm if you have electric heating) of insulation material – glass fibre is probably the best value. If you do it yourself it might cost around £70 for a three-bedroom semi, but you might get two-thirds of that from the local council if the house is yours (see page 175). You could save 20p in every pound of your fuel bill, so if your heating costs you £200 a year you would save the cost of the roof insulation in about two years. After that you make a profit.

Install cavity wall insulation if you can. It isn't a DIY job and may cost £200 to £400 for a semi-detached house, but you could save another 20p in the pound off your heating bill. Make sure that the firm you employ has an Agrément Board Certificate or undertakes to comply with the British Standards. If you have solid walls the insulation will be far harder – it might be more economical just to put aluminium foil behind all the radiators to bounce the heat back into the room, and make sure the rest of your insulation is good.

Double glazing for the whole house could easily set you back £250 even if you do it yourself. If you keep your living room warm most of the time, it is worth double glazing that. If you do it yourself you should get your money's worth in five or ten years – and the house will feel more comfortable, and be quieter.

Curtains and carpets can cut your heat loss a lot if they are good and thick – in really cold weather a blanket over the window may not be very smart, but it will save money much sooner than double glazing will.

2 Control   Insulation will only save you money if you turn down the heaters – otherwise you'll simply be hotter than before but use just as much fuel. The idea of heater controls is to give you the amount of heat you need, when you need it.

A time switch fitted to your central heating could pay for itself in a year. Make sure you set it to turn the heat on *before* you get up or come home, and off *before* you go to bed or go out; that way you will always be greeted with warmth, but not waste heat on an empty or sleeping house. You can fit time switches on some solid fuel and electric storage heater systems, but the effect won't be so great.

Thermostats are usually fitted on central heating boilers, but one for each room or radiator as well will stop any of them getting hotter than you need. They only cost £10 or so each, and should save you that much in two or three years.

Turn down the heating by 1°C and you could cut 8p in the pound off your heating bill. *But* if you are elderly, or if there are babies or ill people in the house, never let the house get cold.

Turn off the heating at night, unless you are elderly, ill or have very young children. It is much cheaper to use more blankets, a hot-water bottle or an electric blanket.

Turn off fires in rooms you aren't using, and shut the door so that the rest of the house stays warm (*but* don't let any room get so cold that the pipes freeze).

Efficient heaters give you more heat for the same amount of fuel – for example, gas 'log' fires can use twice as much as ordinary gas radiant convectors; always ask about efficiencies.

Heating water

If you have central heating, you will pay for your hot water along with your heating (unless you have a separate water heater for the summer), but your hot water may be using as much as a quarter of your fuel. There are lots of easy ways to cut this down:

1 Insulate   There is no point in heating water just to let it get cold again, nor in heating it with expensive day-rate electricity when night-rate is there for the asking.

Lag your tank with at least 80 mm of lagging material. A well-designed tank jacket this thick, and made to the British Standard, will cost under £10, and you could save anything from £20 a year, if you have gas central heating, to three times that much if you use full-rate electricity. If your immersion heater makes the airing cupboard warm, then it's not properly lagged; it would be cheaper to get an airing cupboard heater to do the job.

Lag the pipes that come from the tank – all the cold water that you have to run off before the tap runs hot, was heated once!

2 Control   There is no point in insulating and then having more hot water at a higher temperature than you really need.

Fit thermostats to keep the water temperature to 60°C

(140°F) or 65°C (150°F) which is quite hot enough and actually safer for old people and young children. Electric immersion heaters come with thermostats; you will have to buy one for other heaters. They cost about £30, plus installation, but it should pay for itself in four years or so. Remember, if you always add cold water, your hot water is too hot.

Get a time switch for immersion heaters, and use it to turn on the hot water early enough to give you hot water when you get up without having it all night. Always set it to take advantage of the cheap night-rate electricity. You could save the £18 or so it will cost you in only a year or two.

Use a shower, which only takes a quarter as much water as a bath.

Don't heat more than you need to do the job in hand. If you just need to wash up, use a kettle rather than heating a thirty-gallon tank. Better still, if you have an immersion heater get a second element fitted at the top, or a 'one shot' unit for heating extra hot water during the day. It may cost you between £30 and £50, but if it means you don't keep heating the whole tank at the full day rate, it could save you that much in only a year.

3 Choose your water heater   Very often you have to make do with what is there, but if you can choose, consider the following.

Instantaneous gas multi-point heaters are the cheapest to run. They cost more than electric immersion heaters to buy, but you should save the extra cost in five years, or less if you use gas for heating and cooking too.

Immersion heaters are the next best choice, so long as you run them on cheap night-rate electricity and have a well-lagged tank – preferably holding fifty gallons so you never need a day-rate top up.

With central heating you may want a separate water heater for the summer so that the kitchen doesn't get too hot. If you use the central heating for summer hot water, make sure that there is a valve to stop the hot water being wasted in the central heating system. If you are on the

Economy 7 electricity tariff, it may be cheaper to heat your water by electricity, particularly during the summer, rather than using a gas, oil or solid fuel central heating boiler. Your local showroom should be able to help you with the sums.

Cooking

Cooking is not expensive. Even with an expensive fuel it is unlikely to cost much more than £1 a week for a family of four. What is more, a good hot meal can be a much cheaper way of warming yourself up than sitting in front of a fire. Even so, you can certainly save money by choosing and using your cooker wisely.

1 Choose the right cooker If you have any choice, remember that gas cookers cost more than electric ones to buy, but if you use gas for heating as well, they can cost as little as half as much to run.

2 Beware of second ovens You will probably pay more to buy a two-oven cooker, but don't assume that the smaller oven will save you money by being cheaper to run. Some are not at all well insulated, particularly if you buy an older model second-hand; always find out about the running costs of any oven before you buy.

3 Cook economically It sounds easy, but we often forget. Use lids on pans, make sure pans fit the rings, don't overcook vegetables, and where possible cook all the vegetables together or get a saucepan with separate compartments. Don't keep opening the oven door to have a look, and try not to use the oven for only one dish. Often there are alternative ways of cooking the same thing – for example, you could bake a pound of sausages for 1·12 units of electricity, grill them for 0·36 units, or fry them for only 0·19 units. Two other tips: an electric toaster is cheaper for a couple of slices of toast than the electric grill of your cooker, and an electric kettle is cheaper than a kettle heated on an electric cooker ring. Finally, pressure cookers, although they are expensive to buy, really can save a lot of fuel, because they are so fast. For example, a beef casserole that used 1·16 units of electricity in an oven would only take 0·85 in a pressure cooker, and a steamed pudding that took 1·06 units boiled on top of the stove would only take 0·45 in a pressure cooker. So if your family likes dishes that take a lot of cooker time, a pressure cooker would be a good investment.

Lighting

This costs even less than cooking and isn't really worth worrying much about, but there's no need to be wasteful.

1 Buy the right bulbs Apart from fluorescent tubes, the cheapest way of getting light is to use clear coiled-coil bulbs. If you want a softer light, use pearl rather than opal finish. Long-life bulbs cost more to buy and give you less light for your money; if you need to use them for places where it's hard to change the bulb, make sure you get them with a coiled coil.

2 Use fluorescent tubes These are particularly suitable in kitchens or workshops where looks don't matter so much. They are expensive to buy, but you will save in the end, because they last seven times as long and cost a third as much to run as ordinary bulbs.

3 Don't use thick shades They simply cut off half the light you buy; a thin one can be just as pretty.

Washing

If there are children in the family, your weekly wash could be costing you £1·50 or more. There are ways of cutting the cost, but only by working harder on your washday.

1 Re-use the water in a twin tub This makes it cheaper to run than an automatic.

2 Hang clothes on a line   Any driers, and especially tumble driers, can really add to the cost of your wash.

3 Get a machine with a fast spin   Don't use a tumble drier unless you can afford perhaps an extra £2 a week for the luxury of aired clothes straight from the machine.

4 Wash a full load at a time   Use the shortest, coolest cycle that will do the job.

5 Wash by hand if there isn't enough to fill the machine.

6 Wash during the night if you heat your water by electricity, and are on one of the off-peak tariffs. If that isn't convenient use water heated at the cheap rate and kept hot in a well-lagged tank.

7 Use a launderette if you don't have a lot of washing. The cost is much the same and you won't have to worry about repairs.

Fridges and freezers

Neither of these costs a great deal to run – perhaps £1 a month for a fridge and twice that for a freezer. But while a fridge may almost be a necessity, a freezer certainly is not, and they cost a lot to buy. So think twice before you get one and remember that to make it save you money you will have to work hard at growing, buying and cooking food in bulk. If you do get a freezer, remember the following:

- keep it in the coolest place you can, and never in the kitchen if you can help it;
- keep it full, but not fuller than the maximum recommended by the manufacturer;
- be quick about taking food out and putting it in;
- never put hot or warm food into it;
- defrost it regularly according to the instructions;

– always prepare food for freezing properly – otherwise it could be wasted.

Get a freezer insurance just in case anything does go wrong. Your household insurance policy can include this for only a couple of pounds a year if you ask for it.

In choosing your freezer, remember chest models are cheaper to run; get the biggest one you can afford (at least 0·4 cubic metres per person), so that you can really take advantage of cheap bulk buying; prices vary a lot, so shop around.

All your other appliances

Sewing machines, liquidizers, drills, vacuum cleaners, hair-driers, electric under-blankets, toasters, record players and so on cost so little to run that it really isn't worth bothering about them. However, some of them do cost a lot to buy, so in order to save money try only to get the ones you really need. A sewing machine can save a lot on clothes, especially if you have children; an electric drill could make lots of DIY jobs possible (see page 174), and a toaster is cheaper than using the grill.

When you buy – look at *Which?* (in your local library) to see which model is cheapest, safest and best value. Shop around for the best price – discount stores are almost always cheapest, followed by specialist electrical and domestic appliance shops. At sale times it is worth looking in department stores and gas and electricity showrooms too; remember there's nothing wrong with sale stocks unless you are told about it, and you may get a real bargain.

Final fuel tip

Check your fuel meters at regular intervals – it will soon make you realize how much you are burning, and if you check them before and after insulating or having your own 'save it' campaign, it will encourage you to see how much you have saved. If you aren't sure how to read your meter, ask at your showroom and they will give you a leaflet explaining just how to do it.

Grocery bills

Food probably eats up a quarter of your earnings, so can you cut this down without starving? Food will never be cheap, but shopping wisely will certainly help.

Buying own brands

If you try a supermarket's own brands you may well find there are lots that you like – many are, in fact, made by the same manufacturers as the famous brand names. In October 1979 *Which?* reported that a family of four could save up to 85p a week by switching from leading brands to the cheapest alternative, even in the same shop. If you shop around between shops as well, you might save as much as 20p in the pound. Remember that the own-brand may not always

Don't buy a lot till you know if you like it.

be the cheapest; look out for any special offer and give it a try, but don't buy a lot until you know you like it!

Choosing your supermarket
It usually takes too long to go to one supermarket for some things and another for others, so try sticking to some general rules:

- voluntary chains of shops tend to be more expensive for groceries, though not for fresh food;
- hypermarkets are very cheap, but only if you have one near you, or getting there will cost more than you save;
- vegetables are almost always cheaper in the market outside the supermarket.

Sensible shopping
All shops want you to buy more, and will try in various ways to persuade you.

Never be tempted into buying things you don't need.

Take advantage of special offers, but only on things you know you will use.

Buy larger quantities if it works out cheaper, but only if you will use them up before they go off.

Learn how to compare prices – the trick is to divide the price by the weight, to find the price per pound, gramme, ounce, fluid ounce, or whatever. It takes time to do this so look out for goods which have their 'unit price' marked on them. Some goods aren't marked with their unit price but are always sold in the same size packs so it is still easy to compare prices – things like tea, butter, sugar, and so on.

Always look at the weight rather than the size of the packet and remember that what matters is the *net* weight, not the *gross* weight which includes the packet as well as what's inside it. With most foods it is quite easy to tell which pack gives you most, but it is worth taking a second look at some of the things you buy in the chemist.

Don't buy ready-made meals if you can avoid it.

Make a shopping list so that you aren't tempted by everything you see, but be prepared to buy something you had not planned on if it is a really good offer on something you will use.

Cheaper ways to eat

Cheaper food can be just as good for you – sometimes better! So it pays to learn a bit about nutrition and to take a bit of time over the family's meals.

Meat Cheap cuts need longer cooking. Any saving you make will be burnt up in extra fuel unless you make sure you have a full oven whenever it is on, and maybe use a pressure cooker.

Offal This can be very cheap, and it goes a long way; it is also full of iron and protein. If you aren't too keen, try it with plenty of onion or tomato sauce.

Poultry This is usually cheaper if you get bigger birds and more expensive if you get portions. If you have a freezer, eat half and freeze half; otherwise roast, make a casserole of the remains, and never forget the soup.

Weight loss All meat will shrink and lose weight while you cook it. A 4 lb (1·8 kg) joint of topside will weigh around 2½ lb (1·1 kg) after roasting, and a 4 lb frozen chicken probably less than 1½ lb (0·6 kg): you can't stop this happening, but it is worth remembering when you are comparing prices. It is also worth remembering that if you make a stew or casserole, all the goodness goes into the gravy, so you don't lose so much.

Fish It is good for you, but apart from herring and mackerel is not cheap. Fish prices vary a lot from day to day, so it is better to wait till you get to the fishmonger before you decide what to have.

Vegetables and fruit   So long as you stick to the things that are in season, you can use vegetables as a very cheap way of stretching your meals. Try not to buy more than you need, but if you have some left over, make soup rather than throw them away.

Bulk buying
Bulk buying doesn't just mean buying the largest pack on the supermarket shelf; it means buying enough to last for months. It is convenient, if you've got the space, because you can forget about lavatory paper, sugar, soap and baked beans for weeks to come. But is it cheaper?

Bulk buying meat   Buying for your freezer can actually cost you *more* if you don't check the quality and make sure you get cuts you will really use. If you join up with friends, you may be able to do better by getting even larger quantities and swapping till you all have the bits you like.

Bulk buying vegetables and fruit   Freezing when they are in season can give you luxuries like strawberries at Christmas, and if you look out for special offers on whole trays or sacks at a time you might save as much as 20p in the pound. Always check the quality before you buy. Remember that if you haven't a freezer, you can preserve the vegetables and fruit by bottling.

Food co-ops   These are groups of people who buy food in really big quantities to make the biggest savings. You might save up to 20p in the pound. You need at least a dozen people, and you need to agree what and how much to buy. Always keep proper records, and remember to include the cost of going to collect the food. The biggest savings will probably be on cereals, rice, pasta, flour, and so on, where you may save as much as 50 per cent. If you can find a meat wholesaler and you all have freezers, you can do well on meat, but you are unlikely to save very much on ready-frozen foods except ice-cream. If you would like to start a food co-op, you can get useful advice from the National Consumer Council, 18 Queen Anne's Gate, London SW1H 9AA.

Entertaining yourself

We all need to relax and have a good time – but that need not mean spending a small fortune.

Television A whole evening in front of a colour TV will only cost pennies in electricity, and even with licence and rental or HP payments the total cost won't be more than 50p or so. Buying a set will cost more than renting to start with; for colour TV it will work out cheaper in the end (sometimes in only two years or so), but you may be able to rent a black-and-white set for so little that it will be cheaper than buying, even in the long run. Some firms offer reduced rates to OAPs.

Record players and tape recorders These use no more electricity than televisions, but you have to add the cost of the records and tapes. Save on these by making good use of your local library.

Drinking It is always cheaper at home, but, of course, you won't have the darts, bar billiards or company. If you go to the pub, always check your change against the price list, which by law must be on show. If you are buying drink to have at home, try any cheap brands of whisky, gin, vodka and rum where you may save quite a lot – but only buy one bottle till you know you like it. Be a bit more careful with drinks like brandy or port where the taste matters more and quality can vary a lot. On the whole supermarkets will give you the cheapest drinks, including wine as well as spirits; but always look out for special offers in other shops too. If you brew your own beer you can have a pint for as little as 7p or so, which will soon save you the few pounds you will have to spend on equipment. Home-made wine needs more space and takes more time, but it will also save you a lot.

Kitting yourself out

Clothes and shoes These can be very expensive, but it is possible to save money. Make your own clothes if you can and go to jumble sales and second-hand shops – but *not* for shoes, especially children's which should always be fitted new.

Save-it tips
Spend money on getting the best quality you can of things you will wear a lot and that won't go out of fashion. Go to sales in expensive shops where the reductions can be very big. There won't be anything wrong with the goods unless the label says so.

Don't get clothes that have to be dry-cleaned, which adds a lot to the cost.

Always make quite sure things fit, otherwise they will be a complete waste of money; never buy shoes at the end of a long hot shopping trip when your feet will be bigger than usual.

Mail order
This can certainly save you money if you use it in the right way:

- stick to branded goods where you can check the prices against those in the shops;
- don't pay cash – you won't get a discount so you might just as well spread the cost over as long as they give you.

Mail order catalogues have a reputation to keep up and you are unlikely to get poor quality goods; but beware of fantastic bargains in newspapers and magazines – nothing is ever given away.

Keeping in touch

Telephone charges and stamps can now make keeping in touch with your friends an expensive business; but if you are careful you should be able to save quite a few pounds:

- post letters early enough to only need a second-class stamp;
- if you're sending presents, get light ones;
- make as many of your phone calls as you can after 6 p.m. or at weekends, and never between 9 a.m. and 1 p.m. if you can possibly help it;
- make a note of what you want to say and try not to chat!;
- when you write letters, say all you possibly can, so you won't have to use another stamp for a while.

If you find you are in real difficulty over paying your telephone bill, *don't* just leave it unpaid. Get in touch with the area office manager, whose number is in the front of your telephone directory. Better still, make sure of being able to pay the bill by buying special £1 or £5 stamps at the post office as you go along.

6 Live now, pay later

It often seems as if everyone is ready to lend you money: banks, building societies, shops, credit card companies, not to mention the less respectable lenders, all offer to let you have the goods now and pay for them later. All these lenders are in business for profit and you can be ninety-nine per cent certain that if you pay later rather than now, you will pay more; the only questions are 'How much more?', and 'Can you afford it?'. The answers can make the difference between financial suicide and prosperity.

First principles

Borrowing is perfectly sensible if:

1 You know exactly how much *all* your repayments add up to each week or month – never commit yourself to more than you know you can manage. Fifteen per cent of the money in your pocket (*after* paying the rent or mortgage) is as much as anyone should commit themselves to in debt repayments.

2 You know exactly how much extra you are paying for the privilege of borrowing, and never agree to pay a higher interest rate than is reasonable. Look at what the banks are charging (they put notices up in their windows so you can easily see), and if any lender asks you to pay a great deal more than that, refuse.

3 You never, ever, borrow to repay a debt you already have outstanding.

4 You only borrow for things you really need – and can afford – or that will save you money if you have them.

Working out the cost of credit

The costs of different loans are given in different ways. In order to compare them, and to know what you are really paying, you need to be able to work out the 'true rate' of interest. If you borrow £100 to be repaid in twelve monthly instalments of £10 each, you will end up paying a total of £120. Thus the interest on your £100 loan is £20 and the 'flat rate' of interest (which may be given as the 'rate per annum') is 20 per cent. But after a month you will have paid back some of the loan and by the last instalment you won't owe anything at all. On average over the year you owe just over £50; so your £20 interest is nearer to 40 per cent or about twice as much as the flat rate. The more frequent your repayments are, the higher the true rate of interest is compared to the flat rate. For example, a loan at a flat rate of 14 per cent repaid in four quarterly instalments equals a true rate of 23·6 per cent whereas repaid in fifty-two instalments it equals 30 per cent. However, since October 1980 most credit advertisements are legally bound to tell you the true rate of interest, thus making comparisons easier: be sure you make them.

The costs of different loans are given in different ways.

Finding the cheapest loan

People who lend money charge more to borrowers who they think are a risk. You will stand a better chance of getting a cheap loan if you:

- have a regular job;
- don't have too many other commitments (especially other loans);
- always repay debts on time, so that you have a good record;
- can provide some sort of security – which means things like unit trusts, a life assurance policy or shares – that could be sold to pay off the debt if need be.

Even if you don't think you stand a very good chance of getting a cheap loan, it is always worth trying the cheapest place first – you can only be turned down.

Interest rates vary from time to time, but they generally move up and down together and stay in the same order. From the cheapest to the most expensive the order is:

building society mortgage
insurance policy loan
bank overdraft
bank ordinary loan
bank personal loan
credit cards
HP and credit sale
finance company personal loan
trading checks
moneylenders, pawnbrokers, tallymen

Obviously a mortgage is by far the cheapest, but you can't get a mortgage to pay for a holiday or a new television. For the best deal on every loan, you need to know *where* to go for *which sort* of loan.

Mortgages

These are for people buying houses and cost even less than the rates given because you will almost always get tax relief.

Save-it tip

If you already have a mortgage and need to borrow some money, you can ask the building society if they will 'top you up'. They will be most likely to agree (and you will get tax relief on the extra) if the loan is to build a garage, put in central heating or do any other big home improvement. They are unlikely to lend you any money just because you're short of cash! So if you want to build a garage *and* buy a car, but only have enough cash for one, use the cash for the car and go to the building society for a loan with tax relief for the garage.

Bank overdrafts

You can only get a bank overdraft if you have a bank current account. Having an overdraft means you can go on drawing money out of your account after it is empty! *Never* do this without asking the bank manager first, otherwise he may 'bounce' (refuse to pay) your cheques, and charge you extra. If your bank manager agrees to let you have an overdraft he will set a limit – perhaps a couple of hundred pounds. You must keep inside this limit – overdrafts are meant to help you over a short-term shortage of cash, not to allow you to live beyond your means.

Advantages

1 You pay interest only on what you actually borrow, so if you can pay off a bit you will pay less interest.
2 As loans go, they are cheap.
3 You can use the money for whatever you like – although your bank manager may be more sympathetic if you need a loan to pay the gas bill than if it is for a holiday in the Bahamas.

Disadvantages
1 Your bank manager *can* ask you to pay back the whole loan at any time – though he is unlikely to.
2 You will probably pay bank charges as well as the interest.
3 You may only be able to get one if you can provide some sort of security and are a good customer of the bank, particularly when money is tight in the economy in general.
4 You can't get tax relief, whatever the money is for.

Bank ordinary loans
These are usually for quite large sums of money and you will probably be asked to provide security of some sort. Ordinary loans are normally given for a specific purpose – like building an extension – and have to be repaid in regular instalments over an agreed length of time, which might be as much as five years.

Advantages
1 They are quite cheap.
2 You can get tax relief if the loan is for improving your home – ask your bank manager.

Disadvantage
1 You almost certainly need to provide security.

Bank personal loans
These are more common than ordinary loans and are usually for smaller amounts. Like ordinary loans they are given for a particular purpose – like buying a washing machine – and are repaid in regular instalments over an agreed length of time. The big difference though is that the interest rate is fixed when you take out the loan – which is good if interest rates then rise, but annoying if they fall; so try not to take out a personal loan when interest rates are high.

Advantages
1 The rate of interest is fixed so you know exactly where you stand.
2 You probably won't be asked to provide security.
3 You can't be made to repay the loan before the agreed time is up, and you will normally have at least a year.
4 If you run into difficulties with meeting your repayments you may be allowed longer in which to pay back the loan.

Bank borrowing tip
If you want a loan from your bank, go and talk to your bank manager. If you tell him exactly what you need the money for and how long you will need to repay the loan, he will advise you on which of the various sorts of loan will be best.

Insurance company loans
If you have got a 'whole life' or 'endowment' life assurance policy with a 'cash-in' or 'surrender' value, you may be able to borrow from the insurance company on the strength of it. You can usually borrow up to ninety per cent of the cash-in value, which, of course, can be more the longer you have had the policy. You won't usually have to pay the loan back until the policy matures (that is when the money is paid out) and when that time comes the money will be there. It is really just a way of having the cash before the date originally agreed.

Advantages
1 It is fairly cheap.
2 You know for certain that you will have the money to pay back your debt – all you have to do is find the interest in the meantime.

Disadvantage
There may be a high minimum charge, which can make this an expensive way of getting a short-term loan. If you only

want to borrow for a short time, it would probably be better to use your insurance policy as security for a bank loan.

Credit cards

Many people now have Access or Barclaycards, which allow you to sign for goods and services up to a personal limit (for example £300) and pay one bill to the credit card company at the end of the month. If you use your card carefully you can borrow for a short time without paying any interest at all; but if you borrow for too long the cost can become quite high.

Advantages

1 So long as you pay off your whole debt within twenty-five days of the statement date each month, you pay no interest at all.
2 It's an easy way of paying for things without having to worry about carrying cash about or risking putting your bank account into the red.
3 You can use your card in a great many shops, restaurants, garages, and so on, for whatever you want to buy.
4 You don't have to have a bank account to get a card – just ask in a bank for an application form.

Disadvantages

1 Credit cards can be expensive if you don't pay in full each month – well above the cost of a bank overdraft if you let the debt run on for a whole year.
2 They make it very easy to spend money, which may be more of a temptation than is wise.
3 Unlike a cash loan, you can't use them in all the places you may want to, but only where you see the sign; and if you use them to borrow cash you don't get the interest-free twenty-five days, so you pay interest right from the start.

Finance company personal loans
These are usually offered by tradesmen who are selling you
something big, like a car. You usually pay a fixed rate of
interest, and pay the loan back over a period of up to three
years. Occasionally you may be able to borrow straight from
the finance company, some of which now have High Street
branches, but this is much less common.

If a tradesman offers you a finance company loan,
remember it is *not* the same as HP, although you pay instalments in much the same way. The difference is that you own
the goods from the start, whereas with HP you don't own
them till you pay the last instalment. This means that with a
personal loan you can always sell the goods if you can't
keep up the payments or decide you don't want the thing
after all. With HP you will have to pay for the goods in the
end, or have them taken away from you.

Advantages
1 It is usually cheaper than HP or credit sale.
2 The rate of interest is fixed from the beginning, so you
  know exactly where you are – and if interest rates rise you
  will not be hit.
3 You probably won't have to provide any security.

Disadvantages
1 If other interest rates fall, you will have to go on paying
  at the rate fixed when you obtained the loan; try not to
  take out these loans when interest rates are high.
2 If you fall behind with your payments, you may be asked
  to pay the whole debt off at once. If you think you may be
  getting into difficulties with the repayments, tell the
  finance company at once; don't wait till the last minute.
  If they know what the problem is they are more likely to
  be sympathetic and give you longer to pay.

Hire purchase

Hire purchase means just what it says – you hire the goods until the very last payment, when they finally become yours. Although the loan will be arranged by the tradesman from whom you are buying the goods, you will, in fact, almost always be borrowing the money from a finance company, and it will be the finance company – not the shop – who really own the goods. Make sure you know the name and address of the finance company, because it is with them that you should get in touch if you have difficulties with your repayments. They are also responsible along with the shop if the goods you buy turn out to be faulty.

If a shop which offers HP refuses to let you have a loan, it is probably because the finance company thinks you are a bad risk; this may be true, in which case there is nothing you can do about it, or it may be a mistake that you can put right (see page 108, 'Keeping your record clean').

If you are under eighteen, you will almost certainly be asked to provide a 'guarantor'. This is someone who will pay your debt for you if you can't manage it. This is a big favour to ask of anyone, and if you are asked to be a guarantor, remember that in law you are responsible for repaying the loan, so think twice before you agree.

If you fall behind with your HP payments, tell the finance company at once. In theory they may be able to take the goods away, but in practice they are more likely to give you longer to pay up.

Advantages

1 A lot of shops offer HP and make all the arrangements for you.

2 If you have paid more than a third of the total price, including interest, and then get into difficulties with your repayments, the finance company will have to go to court before it can get the goods back. The court may well allow you to repay the loan over a longer time.

3 If you decide you don't want the goods or can't afford them, you can return them whenever you like; *but* you

may have to pay half the total purchase price come what may, so don't give the goods back till halfway through the time of the loan.
4 The rate of interest is fixed when you first sign the agreement, so you always know just where you are; but of course this makes HP a bad sort of loan to take out when interest rates are high.

Disadvantages
1 Unless you are buying something essential like a cooker or a fire, you will have to find a deposit out of your own pocket.
2 Interest rates vary from shop to shop, and it is not always easy to tell which is the cheapest.
3 The goods are not yours until the last payment, so you cannot sell them.

Credit sale
You might confuse this with HP, because it is offered and arranged by shops in much the same way, and you pay instalments in much the same way too. The big difference is that you own the goods from the beginning, so they can't be taken away from you even if you fall behind with the repayments. It is important to be clear which sort of loan you have got.

Advantages
1 If your agreement is to pay the whole debt off in less than nine months you may not have to pay a deposit.
2 You can sell the goods whenever you like, though if you do you may have to pay the finance company at once too.
3 The goods cannot be taken away from you.

Disadvantage
1 You cannot return the goods to the finance company if you decide you don't want them or can't afford them after all.

Shop credit accounts
Some shops will let you run up a bill till the end of the month, when you pay the whole lot at once. Often they don't charge you any extra for this sort of credit. If you do a lot of your shopping at one shop, and can arrange to pay the bill when you get paid, it can make it much easier to find the cash, and is very convenient. *But* don't be tempted into buying more than you can really afford, just because you haven't got to pay up on the spot. Another sort of shop credit account, often offered by department stores, works rather like Access or Barclaycard, and costs about the same. Again, don't be tempted to overspend.

Budget accounts with shops
These are most common in department stores. You pay a fixed amount every month, perhaps £10, and are allowed to have goods worth up to, say, ten times that amount.

Advantages
1 If your income is low and you can't provide any security, this may be the only sort of loan you can get without resorting to lenders who charge enormous rates of interest.
2 If you keep on paying regularly every month you may be allowed to have a credit account, which is usually cheaper.

Disadvantages
1 You normally pay a service charge rather than interest, and it often works out to be more expensive than a credit account.

2 You are limited to the one shop – so choose one with a good range.
3 You may have to continue your monthly payments even if your account is in credit; so make sure you understand the conditions before you sign on the dotted line.

Check trading
You buy a check from a check trading company or a shop that accepts them. They can be worth up to £30, and you pay for them in weekly instalments, plus interest; these will usually be collected from your door.

Advantages
1 It is an easy sort of loan to get if you haven't got much money – although they are much less common in the south of England.
2 The repayments are collected from you each week.

Disadvantages
1 It is very expensive – perhaps four times as much as a bank loan.
2 You can only use the checks in certain shops.
3 Some check trading agents may tempt you to borrow more than you can really afford.

Catalogue mail order
Although you can pay cash for goods in mail order catalogues, it is really a type of credit. You won't pay any less if you pay cash, so you might just as well have the extra time in which to pay. Prices vary, and it is best to stick to branded items where you can compare the catalogue price with prices in the shops.

Advantages
1 It is very convenient.
2 You may get bargains.
3 You can usually return the goods and have your money back if you don't like them or decide they aren't worth the money. Always check on whether you can return them *before* you send off for goods.
4 If you become an agent you will earn a commission that will make what you buy much cheaper.

Disadvantages
1 You may not be able to get exactly what you want.
2 You may be tempted to overspend.
3 Some things cost a lot more than in the shops.

Credit unions and small loan societies
There are few of these around, but if you can find one they are very good places to go for a loan. They are groups of people with something in common – a tenants' association, for example – who put money into a joint pool and give loans out of the pool to members. The loans are not usually very big, nor for very long periods of time.

Advantages
1 Because they are run by members for members, rather than for profit, the interest rates are low.
2 For the same reason anyone who gets into difficulties with their payments is likely to get a sympathetic hearing.

You can find out about joining, or starting, a credit union from the National Federation of Credit Unions or the Credit Union League of Great Britain (see address list).

Lenders you should not go to
Some people and organizations that offer loans are best avoided, even if you need to borrow very badly indeed. They

often try to lend money to people who need it badly and who are therefore prepared to pay almost anything in the future in order to get hold of some cash now. If you ever find yourself in this sort of position the answer is definitely not to borrow – you can be certain that anyone willing to lend to you will make you pay heavily.

Second mortgages

A mortgage is a loan secured on your house, which means that anyone lending you money on a mortgage can sell your house to get his money back if you fail to pay your debt. Obviously you have to be very careful from whom you borrow money under such conditions. A building society that is a member of the Building Societies Association will be quite safe – which means any of the big names and many of the smaller ones too. A High Street bank will be quite safe too, and may insist on a second mortgage if they lend you a big sum of money – to install central heating, for example. There are, however, much less respectable lenders who offer to lend money to people in financial trouble in return for a second mortgage. They do this in the hope that their client will fail to pay up, in which case they will be able to take possession of the house. So, *never* allow anyone except the big building societies or banks to have a second mortgage on your house.

Tallymen

These are travelling salesmen who call on their customers each week to sell them goods and collect instalments for goods already bought. You may not be asked to pay very much each week, but you will certainly pay a lot more than the goods are worth in the end. It can be very hard to keep track of how much you have paid and how much you still owe, because the tallyman will keep selling you more things, which increases your debt again. It is also very easy to be tempted into buying more than you can afford. Tallymen are best left alone.

Moneylenders

Moneylenders will lend money to people who can't get a loan from anyone else at all. They charge a lot for doing so – *eight* times as much as a bank would be quite possible. If you need to get some extra money so badly that you even think about this sort of loan then you should take a long hard look at your income and expenditure and see what has gone wrong. It is almost impossible that borrowing from a moneylender will help; in fact you will almost certainly get into even worse debt than before. If you are in this sort of trouble, go to your CAB.

Pawnbrokers

A pawnbroker only lends you money if you leave something with him that he could sell if you failed to repay the loan. The more valuable the object you leave with him, the more he will lend you. You must repay the loan in full within six months if you want to be sure of getting your property back. You don't have to pay interest, but it is still better not to borrow from pawnbrokers; if you need the money for more than six months you will do better if you sell your property yourself; and if you only need a short-term loan it would be better to avoid any risk and find the money in some other way. Only consider going to a pawnbroker if you just need a loan to tide you over till pay day – and make sure that the first thing you do with your pay is to go and retrieve your property.

Door-to-door lenders

If anyone calls on you at home uninvited, and offers to lend you money or to introduce you to someone who will lend you money, they are committing an offence. Never have anything to do with such offers. However, people selling goods or services door-to-door *are* allowed to offer you credit to help you buy goods or services from them, so long as they are licensed under the Consumer Credit Act. Always ask if they have a licence, and don't be tempted to buy more than you can afford.

Keeping your record clean

It may seem unfair, but the more money and property you have the easier it will be to borrow more. If you have a steady job and have always repaid loans before, you shouldn't find it very hard to borrow reasonable amounts at fair rates of interest. Though if you are already in debt you will probably only be able to get such an expensive loan that you make your problems even worse. In fact, if you can only get an expensive loan, the chances are that you are thought to be a bad risk and quite likely not to repay your debts; if this is true, then for your own sake you shouldn't try to borrow at all. You might be refused a loan by all the respectable lenders although you really can afford it. This can happen if you have a bad record at a 'credit reference agency'. These agencies collect information about bad debtors from debt collectors, finance companies and County Court records. When you ask to borrow money, the lender can ask a credit reference agency for information about you to help him decide whether you are a bad risk. If you are turned down for a loan, ask the lender if he went to a credit reference agency for information about you. If he did he must tell you which one, and you have a legal right to a copy of the information it has on you. Of course, what it says may be true, but if it is not, then you can put it right. For example, Mr B wrote in to *Money-Go-Round* because he had been refused HP for a washing-machine he wanted to buy. He was upset because 'I have never had any HP before and never been in debt.' It turned out that someone else had given Mr B's address when he was taken to court for not paying his tax. When Mr B explained all this to the finance company they sorted out their records and cleared his name.

Avoiding debt before it happens

Once you have borrowed more than you can afford it will be very hard to get out of debt again. You are running a risk of this if:

- you can't pay one bill or instalment before the next one is due;
- you have borrowed money from lots of different places at the same time;
- you are asking for longer term loans than you used to.

When things begin to go wrong

If you think your debts are mounting up, do something quickly before things get any worse:

1 If your total repayments are less than 15 per cent of the money in your pocket after paying the rent or mortgage, you should be all right in the end. To solve the short-term problem, ask to have a longer time to repay in, reorganize payments and bills so that they don't all have to be paid at the same time of the month, and look at your budget to see where you could make some savings.

2 If your repayments come to more than this, you must do something immediately to stop things getting any worse. Do all that you would to get over a short-term problem, but work out how to cut down your spending or increase your income as well. It may be easiest to economize really hard for a few months to get back on to an even keel, rather than to make half-hearted attempts all the time.

3 Don't borrow another penny until you have paid back at least some of what you already owe.

4 Make sure you are getting all the help you can from the social security.

If things go badly wrong

1 Tell the lender you can't meet the repayments, and explain why not. He will almost certainly prefer to give you longer to pay in than have the nuisance of taking you to court.
2 Never just stop paying; you could be sued and end up paying all the legal costs as well as what you owe already.
3 Remember that unless you have the goods on HP, they are yours and can't be taken away.
4 If you get a notice from a County Court or are being harassed by a debt collector, go to your CAB for help.
5 If you are taken to court, don't panic. The court may work out an arrangement for you to pay over a longer time, and it certainly won't make you pay an impossible amount all at once.
6 If the court decides against you, you will have to find the money. If this takes you more than twenty-eight days, make sure you tell the court in writing when you finally do pay, and ask for a Certificate of Satisfaction. If you don't do this your name will go into the court records and you may land up in the files of a credit reference agency as a bad debtor.

If you are asked to pay too much

Interest rates are not fixed by law, but there is a law against 'extortionate' credit agreements. If you think that you are being asked to pay an unreasonably high rate of interest, or that any of the terms of your agreement are unfair, you can ask a County Court to decide whether your agreement is extortionate, in which case you may get back some of the interest you have paid.

7 Saving and investing

It is always a good idea to save a bit of your income, regularly if you can. Then, if something unexpected happens, like a new arrival in the family or the car giving up the ghost, you will be able to cope quite easily; and you won't need to worry so much about the occasional big planned expense, a holiday, perhaps. If you arrange your budget carefully (see Chapter 3) you may well be able to put aside a little bit each week or month without it hurting much. Then when you need some extra cash you'll be surprised at how much all those little bits have added up to.

As your savings begin to grow, you will want to decide where to keep them – and an old sock under the mattress is not the best place. Not only is it easily stolen, and easy to spend, but it is a waste not to take advantage of one of the many savings schemes which can make your savings grow. At the moment the value of money is falling fast, so unless

As your savings begin to grow.

you make your savings earn interest you will quickly find that they are worth a lot less than you thought.

There are savings and investment plans to suit every possible saver. But until you've saved quite a lot – perhaps two months' total earnings – you should stick to the schemes that are absolutely safe. Other schemes *might* give you a better return, but they might *not*; and until you have plenty to spare you can't afford to take any risks. It is also important to keep some of your savings where you can easily get at them at a moment's notice. Again, you might get a higher return if you promised to leave your money in a scheme for a number of years, but you should only go in for that sort of commitment when you've saved plenty to cover emergencies.

Which schemes are absolutely safe?

Your savings will be completely safe in the following places:

National Savings – National Savings Bank (which used to be the Post Office)
  – Savings Certificates
  – Retirement Issue Savings Certificates
  – Save As You Earn
  – Premium Savings Bonds
Trustee Savings Banks
Local Authority loans
Building societies belonging to The Building Societies Association

What sort of saver are you?

Before looking at any particular way of saving, you must decide what sort of saver you are. If you think about the following questions, you will get a good idea of the sort of scheme you should be looking for.

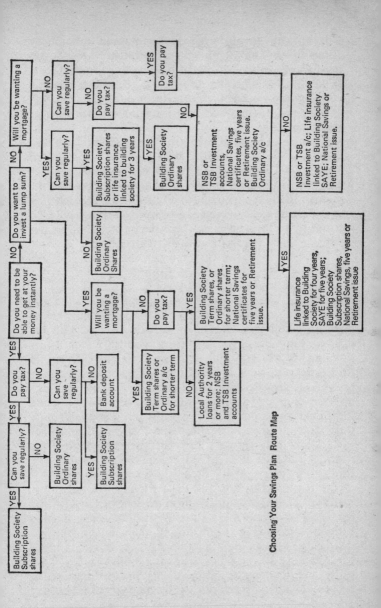

Choosing Your Savings Plan Route Map

1 Do you want to put aside the same amount of money regularly every month, or would you rather be able to put in whatever you can spare, whenever you can spare it?

2 If you have a lump sum to invest – a golden handshake perhaps – do you want to get an income from it, or do you want to put it somewhere where it will grow into a bigger lump sum still?

3 Do you want to be able to get at your savings at a moment's notice, or a month's notice, or are you happy to leave them where they are for a number of years?

4 Do you pay income tax? This is important, because the taxman treats the income from different savings schemes in different ways. If you are a taxpayer you would do better to go for a scheme where the income is either not taxed at all or at least taxed at less than normal.

If you can save regularly for five years

The *National Savings Save As You Earn* scheme is the first choice if you can save regularly for five years and want to build up a nest-egg, whether or not you pay tax. You can put in any number of whole £s from £4 to £20 a month, and as long as you keep putting in the same amount each month for five years all your contributions will be revalued to keep up with the increase in retail prices. You are allowed to miss up to six monthly payments – although you will have to add them on at the end of your five years; but if you miss more than this you cannot make any more payments and your savings will only earn six per cent interest (provided the contract is at least one year old), which is a lot less than you could get from several other schemes. So only start on SAYE if you are sure you will be able to keep it up.

If you can leave your savings in the scheme for a further two years after your five are up, they will be revalued again without your having to put in any more money yourself, and you will get an additional bonus equal to two months' contributions. Again, don't decide to do this unless you are really sure you won't need the money for two more years, because if you take it out during this time you won't get any

114

extra benefit at all. Anyone over sixteen can join the scheme – just ask for a form in the post office or in your bank if you want to pay by standing order – and nobody has to pay tax on their profit.

Remember that this scheme is *not* the same as the SAYE scheme run through building societies. This is also government backed and also involves saving regularly for five years, but it offers variable bonuses rather than index-linking to the retail price increase. In May 1980 the return was only 8·3 per cent or so. The income you get from both is tax-free, and you can save in both SAYE schemes at the same time if you wish.

If you are retired
For anyone over retirement age, whether or not you pay tax, *Retirement Issue National Savings Certificates* ('Granny Bonds') must be the first choice. You only have to keep the certificates for a year, and at the end of that time you will get back enough money to buy as much as the money you saved would have bought if you had spent it at the start. You can buy the certificates in a post office or Trustee Savings Bank for £10 each, whenever you have £10 to spare; but you are not allowed to buy more than £1,200 in the scheme at a time. Provided you keep your certificates for a year or more they will be revalued to keep up with the rise in retail prices; but if you need your money back in less than a year you will only get back the number of pounds you put in. If you can leave your savings in the scheme for five years you will get a bonus of 40p for each £10 certificate, on top of whatever it takes to keep up with inflation. All the payments you get are free of United Kingdom income and capital gains tax.

If you have a lump sum to invest and want to turn it into an income for your retirement, an annuity may be the answer. You pay your lump sum into a life insurance company to buy your annuity, and they pay you an income till your death. The older you are when you buy the annuity, the higher the income you will get for any given lump sum, because the insurance company doesn't expect to have to go on paying it for so long. There are several sorts of annuity; some pay out a lump sum when you die, as well as giving you an income until then; some allow you to have your money back after five years; some are for couples, and so on. You should get expert advice before you decide on any annuity. However, if you have a fairly big sum to invest and would pay tax on the income from it if you invested it in some other way, the tax concessions on annuities make them very attractive. The most important thing to check before you decide, is whether or not you can ever get your lump sum back again – with many annuities you can't, and if you had not been aware of this all along, it could come as a blow later on.

If you don't pay tax
If you don't pay income tax there is no point in putting money in schemes that give you a tax-free income. In particular, you should not put your money in a building society, where tax will be deducted from the interest before you get it – and there's no way of getting it back. Mr S wrote to *Money-Go-Round* to ask whether he could get back the tax paid on his building society account for years past. The sad answer was no, although both Mr S and his wife had not paid income tax for years. You should normally go for the higher rates of return offered by one of the following schemes, although, as with all investments, you should compare current rates of interest, and things like convenience, before you finally decide.

1 National Savings Bank Investment Account This will suit you well if you want to be able to put money in whenever you have a bit to spare, and don't mind having to give a month's notice in writing to take it out again. You can open an account in any post office, with anything from £1 upwards, and once you have an account you can take your bank book to any post office you like to put more money in or give notice that you want to take it out. This is a good scheme to set children on the right road to saving, because it is so easy to use, and they are allowed to operate their own accounts as soon as they are seven. Younger children can have accounts opened for them by their parents, but no withdrawals will be allowed until the child is seven. The interest rate in October 1980 was 15 per cent.

2 Trustee Savings Bank Investment Account If you bank at the TSB it may be easier to have your savings in the same place. The scheme is very like the NSB Investment Account.

3 Local Authority loans If you have a lump sum of at least £100, and are sure you won't need it for a couple of years or more, you could do very well with these schemes. Various local authorities have different minimum investments and offer different rates of interest, but usually you will need to put in at least £500 for anything from two to five years or more. It is not just that the rate of return is lower if you need your money back before the time is up, you simply are not allowed to have it back before the due date; so be very careful before you go in for any of these schemes.

The interest rate is high – 15 per cent or more in October 1980 – and it is fixed when you put your money in, so you will do well if you buy while rates are high. Tax is taken off the interest before you get it, so if you don't pay income tax you will have to claim it back.

If you think you can manage the complications of this sort of saving, take a good look at the adverts in the Sunday papers before you decide which local authority to invest in; the rules are different for each, and there is no need to invest in the area you happen to live in.

4 High Street bank deposit accounts If you want to be able to get at your money at a moment's notice and make a good impression on your bank manager at the same time, a bank deposit account could be the place for the savings you put by for emergencies. You don't need to have a current account in order to have a deposit account, but if you are going to have both, then it will be most convenient to have them at the same branch – and it should smooth relations with your bank manager too. You can open an account with any sum of money, and you can put more in whenever you like. You can usually take out as much as you like without giving any notice too, but if you want to take out a big sum it is a good idea to give a bit of warning.

The interest rate on bank deposit accounts varies from time to time so always check that your savings are earning the best possible return. Remember this interest is taxable, so don't keep more than an emergency fund in the bank if you start paying tax.

5 Building society subscription shares If you will be wanting a mortgage in the future you should put some money in a building society now. There may be times when you could invest more profitably, but it will improve your chances of getting a mortgage if you put money into a building society regularly (see below for details). If it will be your first home, then you should register with the government scheme to help first-time buyers (see page 68).

If you do pay tax
If you pay income tax, then any interest you receive from your savings may also be taxed. This means that it may be better to put your savings into one of the schemes for which there are special rules to let you off paying some or all of the tax.

1 Building society accounts If you pay basic rate income tax, then some sort of building society account will suit your needs. The interest is paid to you after having basic rate income tax liability discharged, which means that although you have to fill in what you get on your income tax return, you won't be asked to pay any more unless you pay higher rate income tax. All building society accounts are easy to open and use – you just walk into a building society and say which sort of account you want to have. You will find that there are several sorts of account, with different rates of interest; you will get a higher rate if you agree to save regularly every month or to leave a lump sum in your account for a couple of years or more.

Ordinary share accounts are what more than eight out of ten building society investors have. You can put money in or take it out whenever you like and the interest rate in October 1980 was around 10·5 per cent (basic rate tax paid).

Subscription share accounts are for people who want to save a regular sum each month but do not want to commit themselves to keeping it up for the five years required by the SAYE scheme. You can't take money in and out of a subscription account as you can with an ordinary account, but if you *really* need the money you can usually close the account altogether without losing any interest. The interest rate is about 1·25 per cent higher than on an ordinary account (11·75 per cent in October 1980), and you can normally save between £5 and £20 to £100 a month.

Term shares are for people who have a lump sum of maybe £100 or more that they want to invest for two years or more. You will receive a higher rate of interest the longer you promise to leave your money where it is – perhaps 11·0 per cent for two years, 11·5 per cent for three years and 12·5 per cent for five years; and the interest rate will vary along with the ordinary share rate. You must be quite certain that you won't need the money before the agreed time is up, because you cannot have it back any sooner.

2 National Savings Certificates If you can leave your money where it is for five years, the 19th issue of National Savings Certificates will earn you 10¼ per cent interest on which the tax is already paid for you, even if you pay higher rate income tax – in fact you don't even have to fill in the interest on your tax return. Again, you should be sure you can leave your savings where they are for the full five years, because although you are allowed to cash your certificates in sooner, you will receive a lower rate of interest. The shorter the time you keep your certificates, the lower the return you will receive. If you are uncertain how long you will be able to leave your money, put it where you can get at it, such as a building society ordinary account.

Certificates cost £10 each, and you can buy them in post offices, High Street banks and Trustee Savings Banks. Because they are so easy to buy, do not have to be declared on anyone's income tax return and offer a reasonably high rate of interest, National Savings Certificates make good presents for children. You could get a higher income for your child (if he doesn't have so much money that he has to pay tax) from an investment where the tax is not prepaid, such as an NSB investment account.

3 Life insurance linked to building societies If you are under thirty-five or so, healthy and want to put aside a few pounds a month for four years, and especially if you pay a lot of income tax, you will get a very high return from a life insurance scheme linked to building society shares.

Proposal forms are available from any of the building societies or life insurance offices offering this sort of plan, but it would be a good idea to ask the advice of several before you decide on one – different schemes have different rules and one may suit you much better than another.

You pay a premium every month, part of which buys you life insurance and part of which is invested in a building society. You don't receive interest each month or year, as you do with other building society accounts, but when you want your money back you can cash in the policy and get back your savings plus all the interest at once. Most of the schemes are supposed to last for ten years, but the best moment to cash in your policy is after four years. For higher rate tax payers, these schemes probably offer the highest possible rate of return at around 15 per cent after paying basic rate tax, *but* don't start one unless you are sure you can keep it up for four years – if you needed money after only a year you might actually get back fewer pounds than you had put in, because the cost of setting up the policy could more than eat up the interest. Don't think that one of these schemes will give you all the life insurance you need. If you saved £10 a month the life cover might be £1,800, which is certainly not enough for most family men.

4 National Savings Bank ordinary accounts The first £70 interest each year is free of tax, which at the beginning of 1980 would have been earned on an investment of £1,400. The interest rate is only 5 per cent, but because it is tax-free, this is equivalent to 7·14 per cent for basic rate tax payers, and a nice 12·5 per cent if you pay tax at 60 per cent.

5 Premium Bonds These are a gamble, but the prizes, ranging from £50 to £100,000, are tax-free.

8 Insurance

If you have an insurance policy you pay a small amount to an insurance company each month or year – called a premium – and if the accident or misfortune you have insured against happens then the insurance company pays you, or your family, a sum of money to help put things right. You can insure against all sorts of things, but for most of us the important ones are:

- insurance for the building you live in against fire, flood and storm;
- insurance for the things that belong to you – the contents of your home – against fire, theft, flood, and so on;
- insurance for you and your family, often called life assurance – so that your family will have something to live on if you die young or to provide some extra money when you retire;
- insurance for your car and your passengers while you are driving, in case you have an accident that is your own fault and need to pay repair bills, or compensation to people who get hurt;
- insurance on your holidays in case you are ill, have an accident, lose all your money or your car breaks down and you need to pay for repairs and extra fares, hotels or doctors.
- insurance for when you are ill, so that if you can't go on working there will still be some money coming in.

You may think that none of these disasters will ever happen to you, but they do happen every day. Around two million claims are made each year for damage or loss of property from people's homes and as a result over £200 millions are

House Buildings Insurance

Covered

Damage to the building itself, the windows, baths, lavatory, basins, sinks, plumbing, fitted cupboards, decoration, garage, underground pipes and cables and other permanent fixtures from the mishaps listed below:

- Oil leaking from central heating
- Storm
- Riots and malicious damage
- Explosion
- Lightning
- Falling trees
- Falling TV aerials
- Impact by vehicles
- Subsidence

- Flood
- Fire
- Theft
- Water escaped from tanks and pipes.
- Alternative accommodation while yours is repaired.
- Legal property owner's liability for claims by people hurt by falling bricks, etc.

Not covered

Alternative accommodation costing more than 10 per cent of the total sum insured.
- ☐ The first £15 of storm damage (unless you pay an extra premium)
- ☐ The first £250 of subsidence damage.
- ☐ Riots in Northern Ireland.
- ☐ TV aerials themselves — although any damage they do will be covered.
- ☐ Storm or flood damage to gates and fences.
- ☐ Anything at all if the house is left empty for more than thirty days — before you move in, for example.

paid out by insurance companies. On top of that, over 150,000 motor vehicles disappear every year. So, if you own anything that would cost money to replace, or if you have a family who would find money short if you stopped earning, then you need insurance.

Insuring the building you live in

If you own your home or are buying it on a mortgage then you need to insure the building itself.

How much insurance do you need?
Most companies have tables to help you work it out, but you should know how the sums are done:

1 Measure the total outside floor area, including the garage if it is integral to the house.
2 Ask some local builders, your insurance company, or the British Insurance Association the current cost of building; it will be around £30 per square foot (about £325 per square metre) including clearing rubble and employing a surveyor, but could be quite a lot more in London and the South-East, or Scotland, or if you live in an unusual type of house.
3 Multiply the total floor area (including upstairs floors as well) by the rebuilding cost.
4 Get a policy which is index-linked, or make sure you have added enough on to your valuation to cover two years of inflation.
5 Add perhaps £3,000 for a separate brick-built garage – £4,000 if it is a double garage.

For example, a typical semi-detached home with an attached brick-built garage might have a total floor area of 1,125 square feet, plus the garage. If it is in a medium-priced area such as Greater Manchester, and built between the wars, it might cost £28 a square foot to rebuild, or a total of £34,000.

Do not insure for what the house might cost to buy – if it burned to the ground you would have to rebuild it, not buy it.

Remember that if your house has anything unusual about it – a thatched roof or a luxury fitted kitchen perhaps – it will cost extra to rebuild.

Claims

What can you claim for?
Most policies cover roughly the same things: damage to the building itself and fixed things like baths and cupboards and interior decoration, from misfortunes such as flood, storm, fire, burglars, lightning, vehicles, subsidence, falling trees, or a burst pipe in the plumbing or heating systems.

What can't you claim for?
You won't get anything for normal wear and tear; normal settling or normal maintenance.

Will the insurance company pay the whole bill?
You often have to pay £15 or so towards damage from flood, storm, escaping water, vandals and your own animals or vehicles. You can pay an extra premium of perhaps £5 a year to avoid some of these 'excesses'.

You may have to pay £250 or more towards subsidence damage, and you cannot usually pay an extra premium against this particular risk.

When the insurance company settles your claim, you may get a note saying that the cheque is 'in full and final settlement'. Before you accept this it is important to be certain that there will be no further bills. Mrs G wrote in to *Money-*

Go-Round to ask for advice on this. She had accepted a cheque in full and final settlement for damage from a flood and then found that there was another bill from the storage company where she had stored her furniture while the damage to her floors was repaired. Sadly there was nothing we could do to help because she had accepted the final settlement.

How to claim
Always keep your policy safe – it is useful to have a copy at home but safest to keep the original in the bank. To claim:

1 Tell the police if anything has been stolen, or if there has been any malicious damage.
2 Tell the insurance company at once; give them your policy number.
3 The insurance company will send you a claim form – fill it in and return it as soon as possible.
4 Don't have any repairs done yet; obtain estimates, then wait till the insurance company agrees.
5 If you need emergency repairs, tell the insurance company.
6 If your insurers offer much less than you think they should, write and ask why, and explain your point of view.

How to choose an insurance company?
1 Stick to the well-established companies.
2 Go to three or four companies, ask how much they charge and exactly what their policy covers; the cheapest may not cover all eventualities, or may ask you to pay more excesses.
3 If your house is unusual – thatched, wooden or very old perhaps – shop around even more.

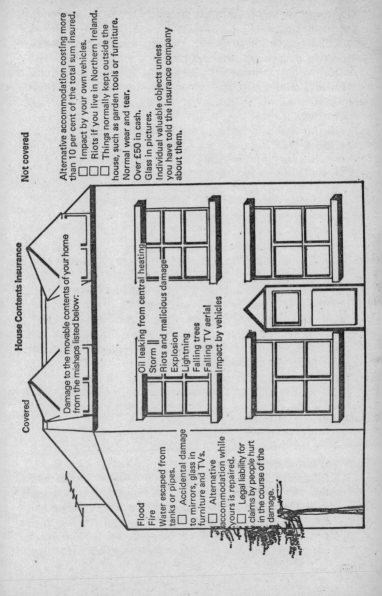

House Contents Insurance

Damage to the movable contents of your home from the mishaps listed below:

Covered

Flood
Fire
Water escaped from tanks or pipes.
- Accidental damage to mirrors, glass in furniture and TVs.
- Alternative accommodation while yours is repaired.
- Legal liability for claims by people hurt in the course of the damage.

Oil leaking from central heating
Storm
Riots and malicious damage
Explosion
Lightning
Falling trees
Falling TV aerial
Impact by vehicles

Not covered

Alternative accommodation costing more than 10 per cent of the total sum insured.
- Impact by your own vehicles.
- Riots if you live in Northern Ireland.
- Things normally kept outside the house, such as garden tools or furniture.
Normal wear and tear.
- Over £50 in cash.
Glass in pictures.
Individual valuable objects unless you have told the insurance company about them.

Moving, renting and new houses

If you move, get insurance on the house you are moving to, from the date you exchange contracts.

If you buy a brand new house you may get a National House Building Council guarantee, but you should get insurance as well because the guarantee only covers bad construction.

If you rent your home your landlord should insure the building itself, but it is a good idea to check. You will need your own contents insurance.

Insuring the things you own

Add up what it would cost to replace every single movable thing in your home, from the bed to the last cup and saucer.

If you want an indemnity policy, take off a bit for wear and tear; for example, if your bed would cost £50 to replace new but is five years old and you expect it to last another five years yet, value it at £25. If you have a 'new for old' policy, you will have to value everything at the amount it would cost to buy it new. Add on 15p in the pound to allow for inflation, or get an index-linked policy.

Remember then, if you insure for less than your property is worth, the insurance company may not be legally bound to pay you a penny, and they will almost certainly pay out less than you ask for.

What sort of policy is best?

An **indemnity policy** could leave you badly out of pocket because it only pays out enough to replace what you lose with property of the same value. If you lost furniture and carpets in a fire, you would either have to replace them with cheap second-hand ones, or make up the difference between their value and the cost of new ones yourself.

A **new-for-old policy** will cost more, but will enable you to replace most of your property with brand new replacements if disaster strikes. Most new-for-old policies will give you new-for-old cover on carpets, furniture, electrical equipment, and so on, but not on clothes or household linen, where wear and tear will be taken into account.

How much will it cost?
This depends on:

- what your belongings are worth;
- what sort of policy you want;
- where you live.

For every £1,000 of cover you might pay around £3 a year for an indemnity policy if you live in the country, but maybe as much as £5·50 in London. A new-for-old policy would probably cost between 50p and £1 more for each £1,000 of cover, and again you will pay more if you live in the middle of a big city or in areas with high crime rates.

Points to remember

Tell the insurers if you own any single valuable thing worth over £500 or whatever is given in your policy as the 'valuables' limit.

Don't keep more cash in the house than the limit allowed in your policy; normally this is £100, but it may be as little as £60.

If your home is not self-contained, or you let part of it, you won't be able to claim for theft unless the burglars had to break in.

Your belongings are covered if you take them out of the house for a time, but not abroad, and usually not in your car, though this may be covered in your motor policy. (If you have any property that you often take out of the house, and want to have insured, ask your insurance company.)

Don't keep your policy where it is likely to be stolen.

Final tips
Raise your cover to keep up with inflation and to include things you buy. Don't claim for *every* tiny accident – your premium may go up.

Life assurance

You *in*sure against things that may or may not happen – such as your house being burnt down; you *as*sure for things that are bound to happen – we are all bound to die in the end. If you have a life assurance policy you pay a smallish sum each month – the premium – and when you die, or when you reach a certain age, your family, or you, are paid by the life assurance company.

Who needs life assurance?
If anyone depends on you for their welfare then you should have a life assurance policy. The state may pay a widow £27·15 a week, plus £7·50 for each child, which is hardly enough to live on. Supplementary benefits or family income supplement will help, but if there is a mortgage to pay and commitments like HP to be met, a widow and any children can be in real trouble. Accidents do happen, and sadly many people do die long before their time. Taking a less gloomy view, some sorts of life assurance policies are good investments and with an 'endowment policy' you can collect the money yourself when you reach a certain age.

Married women should get life assurance too, especially if there are children. If you work, your family could suddenly be deprived of part of its income; and if you stay at home to look after the children then your husband would need extra cash if you were not around, to pay for things you used to provide.

Remember: ten in a thousand men and nearly seven in a thousand women die between the ages of twenty and fifty-four. Seven thousand married women under forty-five die each year, who may very well be caring for children.

What sort of policy?
There are three basic sorts of life assurance:

1 Whole-life policies You pay a premium regularly for the rest of your life, and when you die your family is paid a lump sum. You can pay a higher premium to get a 'with profits' policy – which pays out more when you die.

2 Term policies You pay a regular premium for an agreed number of years – usually ten or more. If you die before that time is up, your family is paid either a lump sum or a monthly income – but if you survive, you get nothing. This sort of policy gives a lot of cover for a small premium, but you may get nothing out of it at all. It is much the cheapest way of protecting your family, one popular variety being the 'mortgage protection policy' which is arranged so that if you should die your family will get just enough to pay off what is left of the mortgage. It is always best to get a 'convertible term' policy, which you could change into an investment type endowment policy whenever you felt you could afford it, without having to have any medical examination.

3 Endowment policies You pay a regular premium for an agreed number of years, often till retiring age. If you die before the time is up your family gets paid, and if you survive, you get paid. You can pay a higher premium for a with-profits policy, which should pay out more in the end. Most endowment policies cost more than term policies because they are investment schemes as well as assurance, but they can be profitable in the end.

Which policy for you?
Your choice depends on:

- what you can afford;
- what sort of family you have;
- how old you are;
- your other investments and commitments.

Guidelines to help you:

Term assurance is best for young people with families and not much spare cash. Tell the life assurance company that you want to protect your family; decide whether it would be better for them to have a regular income or a lump sum of money, and if you have a mortgage make sure there would be enough to repay it. A healthy person in their twenties could probably get £15,000 of cover for as little as £20 a year, so almost anyone can afford it.

Whole-life assurance is for people whose savings and pension will be enough for their own retirement needs, but who would like to leave some money to their family. However, you could probably leave them more by investing your money in some other way (see Chapter 7).

Endowment assurance can be a profitable investment as well as a way of protecting your family. Unless you can only afford term assurance you should get a with-profits endowment policy. You will almost always pay more for your life cover than with a term policy, but you will have a good investment. Your policy may be linked to equities or unit trusts, and the profits will vary so that it is hard to tell which will do best; in fact it is less important to go for one company rather than another than to remember the following:

1 Don't buy a policy if there is any chance that you won't be able to keep up the payments; you can lose a lot if you have to terminate the policy too soon. Mrs B wrote in to *Money-Go-Round* because she had paid £6·35 a week for ten months for an endowment policy which she then found she could not afford to go on with. She had paid

£259 into the policy but, in her own words, 'They said there's no way we will get any money back.' Sadly, this was true. If she had been paying premiums for a number of years, she would have got *something* back, but you should always check on what is called the 'surrender' or 'cash in' value before you decide on a policy.

2 Look at how much life cover you receive. If it is not enough (see next section) and you can't afford a higher premium, then think about a term policy instead, at least for the time being.

How much life assurance do you need?

Your insurance company should help you work it out, but ask yourself these questions:

1 What income would your husband or wife need to live on if you died?
2 What debts would you leave if you died tomorrow? They won't *have* to be paid off, but your partner would have an easier time if they could be.
3 What extras will have to be paid for as the family grows up?
4 What other income will your family have if you die?

When you have decided how much life cover you need, you can decide whether you can afford to invest in an endowment policy or whether a term policy would suit you better for the time being. For perhaps £4 a month you could probably make sure that your family would get an income of £3,000 a year from a term policy that would 'convert' to an investment type endowment policy later if you wanted it to.

5 Remember that inflation will reduce the value of the cover you have, so you will need to increase it as the years go by.

Your bank Most bank managers will advise you, but they will only sell policies recommended or run by the bank. These may not suit your needs best, so make sure you know what you will be getting before you sign anything.

Life assurance companies Many advertise widely, and a local branch will be able to help you. Again they will only sell their own policies, so don't hesitate to ask exactly what you will be getting.

Solicitors and accountants Many act as agents for life companies, but don't get pushed into buying a policy unless you understand why it is right for you. Agents work on commission for single companies and may get a bigger commission for selling you a policy that isn't right for you.

Agents They work for individual companies and may get paid a bigger commission for policies that are wrong for you; think hard before signing, and don't sign if you have not fully understood what you will be paying, what you will be getting and what will happen if you can't keep up the payments.

Brokers They don't work for single firms, so you should get a proper choice of policies *if* he's a good broker. Check that he's a member of the British Insurance Brokers' Association, or is registered with the Insurance Brokers' Registration Council. If you want something a little bit different – if you have health problems or complicated financial arrangements perhaps – a broker may be the best way to get exactly what suits you.

Final points to watch
1 Never start a policy you won't be able to afford to continue; you may get back even less than the premiums you have paid. Some companies are tougher than others; always ask about 'surrender values' before starting, just in case.

2 Never get an endowment or whole-life policy, which is mainly investment, if what you really need is cheap life cover.

3 Remember to increase the amount of life assurance you have, in order to keep up with inflation.

4 If you really cannot keep up the payments, ask to make the policy 'paid up' rather than cashing it in straightaway. This means that you stop paying premiums, and of course the pay-out at the end will be smaller, but you will lose less if you do this than if, like Mrs B, you ask for your money back now.

Insurance for illness

If you work for an employer you will be paying NI contributions, and so if you fall ill you should qualify for state sickness benefit. This is £20·65 a week, plus £12·75 if your wife doesn't earn more than that, and £1·25 for each child. With child benefit as well, a married man with two children would end up with £45·40, and after twelve days he might well get an earnings related supplement of up to £11·78 a week – but even that total of £57·18 is not much if you are used to an income of over £100 a week.

If you are self-employed you do not even get this much, and could be in real trouble if you were ill.

Do you need sickness insurance?
It depends what would happen if you were ill.

1 Look at your budget and see what your weekly spending is. Think what you could cut out, and what you really must have.

2 Compare what you will need with the state benefits you would receive (see Chapter 9).

3 Find out exactly what your employer would pay, and for how long.

4 If you would not have enough – and certainly if you are self-employed – you should get sickness insurance. There are several different sorts, and it is important to get the right one.

What sort of insurance?
Hospital cash plans You pay £20 or £30 a year in premiums, and the company pays you around £5 for each day you spend in hospital.

Only one in ten of us is ill enough to go into hospital, and hospital cash plan policies do not pay anything if you are ill at home. Even if you do go into hospital you will probably be out again in ten days, so you will only get £50. Longer stays are most likely to be in psychiatric hospitals – which these policies don't usually pay out on. All in all, this sort of policy is unlikely to be very much help if you are ill.

Permanent health insurance So long as you are young and in good health, you should only need to pay £15 a year or so in premiums and the insurance company will pay you £20 for each week you are off sick. *But* the payments don't usually start till you have been ill for three or even six months – which luckily most of us are not. Even so, if your employer pays you for a while when you are ill, PHI can be a good back-stop for when that pay ceases.

Save-it tips
Start a policy when you are young and healthy – it can't be cancelled later. It is not worth paying extra to have PHI payments start less than three months after you fall ill. It will cost a lot more and you should be able to get by for that long if you have the emergency savings recommended in Chapter 3. If you are self-employed, you will need PHI, and some extra savings, to tide you over the first few months when, unlike many employees, you won't get any sick pay.

Accident insurance If you have a job where accidents are common this is a good idea. £1 a month should bring a building worker perhaps £15 a week for two years, plus a lump sum if you suffer permanent injury. Ask your employer if he has a scheme – it should be cheaper than getting your own.

Private medical insurance This is different from all the other schemes. You don't get cash to help with the family bills, but you do get private medical treatment. From a medical point of view it won't be any better, but you will not have to wait so long, and you will get more attention and hotel-type comforts. This type of insurance could well cost £7 a week for an average family, unless you can join a low-cost scheme such as a group scheme through your employer. Think hard before you spend money on this, and remember it won't pay for pregnancy, osteopaths or other special treatments that are not strictly medical.

You will get more attention and hotel style comfort.

Insurance for motorists

It is against the law to drive without insurance. The fines are large, not to mention the compensation, court awards and repair bills you might face if you had an accident. There are several sorts of insurance – to suit every need.

Road Traffic Act This pays for claims made by other people who get hurt if you have an accident on a public road that is your fault. It does not pay for damage to your or anyone else's car or other property, so you could still face a big repair bill.

Road Traffic Act cover is not enough unless your driving record is so bad that it is all you can get.

Third party This provides Road Traffic Act cover and also pays for damage you do to someone else's car in an accident that is your fault. A middle-aged driver living in the country with a good driving record, a maximum no-claims discount and only one other person allowed to drive his car, might pay £30–£35 a year.

Third party, fire and theft This pays for:

- claims by people who get hurt if you have an accident;
- repairs to other people's cars and property;
- your own car if it gets stolen or goes up in flames.

You will still have to pay the bill for damage to your own car from an accident that was your fault, but if the car wasn't worth a lot in the first place this will probably cost less than getting more insurance. Our 'perfect driver' would probably pay £40 or so for third party, fire and theft insurance.

Comprehensive insurance This pays for all that third party, fire and theft insurance would pay for and also:

- any accidental damage to your own car;

- damage caused by other people while they are driving your car, so long as they have your permission;
- claims by people you injure while driving other people's cars, so long as you have permission.

If your car is worth more than a couple of hundred pounds you should get comprehensive insurance if you possibly can; it could save you a great deal of money. It will cost quite a lot more than third party, fire and theft, but if you ever get into an accident that causes much damage it will be worth it.

Keeping the cost down
1 Get the smallest, dullest car you can.
2 Keep it parked off the road, in a garage if possible.
3 If only you and (say) your wife, ever drive it, tell your insurers.
4 Get, and keep, a 'no claims discount'. Most companies reduce your premium for each year without a claim, till after four or five years you pay only 40p in the pound of the full premium. If you do claim, you won't lose the whole discount at once, but you will lose the last two steps, and then you will have to earn it again. If your premium starts at £150 a year, you may get it down to £75 after four years. It would then be worth paying for damage that cost less than £100 or so, because if you claimed, your premium would probably go up to £112·50 instead of down to £60, and you would go on paying higher premiums for four years, worth over £90 in all, before you caught up again.
5 If you have an accident that was not your fault you must convince the other person's insurance company. Some companies have 'knock for knock' agreements designed to speed up the settling of claims under which each company pays for damage to the car it has insured, regardless of who was to blame. If you were not to blame, the 'knock for knock' agreement should not affect your no claims discount at all.

Remember that you should tell your insurers if you have an accident, even if you aren't claiming. You won't be penalized if you do tell them but you could be if you don't.

Choosing a policy

The cheapest may not be the best; read the policy carefully to see exactly what it pays for, and where you may have to fork out. Look out for 'excesses', which mean that you have to pay the first part of any claim. They could give you a nasty shock if you hadn't realized they existed. Some, however, are useful in that you may be able to protect your no claims discount if you promise to pay the first part of all claims.

Special motor insurance

1 If you often travel long distances, consider a policy that pays for towing you home (or join the AA 'Relay' scheme).
2 If you tow a caravan or trailer, check that the insurers know, and get insurance for it too.
3 If you could not manage without your car, there are a few policies available which pay for hiring one while yours is off the road.

9 Social security

We often hear about the scroungers, but there are also lots of people who do not claim the benefits to which they are entitled. In 1977, over £300 million of supplementary benefits went unclaimed, and almost two million people didn't claim rent and rate rebates they could have had. One of them was Mr E who wrote to *Money-Go-Round* to ask for help. He asked, 'How can I claim any money? At the moment I have been put on short time and all I am bringing home for myself and my wife and child is £40 a week. I am behind with my rent and only have a week left to pay it in.' We advised Mr E to go to his local social security office, and he got help at once.

Find out which benefits you could get.
Don't be too proud to claim what is due to you.
If in doubt, claim.
If you qualify for two benefits but are only allowed one of them, don't worry, you will get the bigger one.
Don't forget help from local authorities as well as social security (see page 161).
If you know someone who you think needs more help then he or she is getting, ask the social services department at the town hall to send a social worker to sort things out.

If you're out of work

Which benefit?
Unemployment benefit.

Who gets it?

Anyone who is willing and able to work but can't get a job, so long as they have paid enough NI contributions – which you will have done if you were working up till now. You will not get unemployment benefit for up to six weeks if you are dismissed for misconduct, or leave your job of your own accord without just cause.

How much is it?

1 £20·65 a week, or less if your NI record is poor.
2 £1·25 for each child.
3 £12·75 for a wife or other adult for whom you qualify for a dependant's increase – but you may get less if your NI record is poor.
4 An earnings-related supplement – though this is now being phased out.

When is it paid?

1 The basic benefit starts after three days (or longer if your employer paid you a sum in lieu of notice) and is paid for a maximum of one year.
2 The earnings-related supplement starts after two weeks and is paid for a maximum of six months.

How do you claim?

1 Go to your local Jobcentre or employment office on your first day out of work to see if they have a job.
2 If there is no work, go to your local unemployment bene-fit office (under 'Employment, Dept of' in the phone book) on your first day out of work. Take your P45 form, which your employer should have given you, and your NI number, which your employer will be able to tell you if you don't know it.

Can you get any other help?

1 If you are made redundant you should get a redundancy payment (see Chapter 2).

2 When you've been out of work for four weeks you should get a tax rebate if you have paid any. Send your P50 form (which your employer should have given you) to your local tax office and claim a rebate. If you don't have a P50, ask the tax office what you should do.

3 TOPS and Employment Transfer Schemes can allow you money to live on while you learn a new skill, or help with fares if you want to look for a job in another part of the country. Ask at your Jobcentre or employment office.

4 If you have no job and a very low income you may get supplementary benefit (see page 144).

5 If you get supplementary benefit or your income is very low, you may be eligible for free prescriptions, dental treatment and dentures, school meals, milk and vitamins (see page 144).

6 If your income is low in relation to your rent or rates you may receive a rent or rate rebate (see page 53).

7 If you get supplementary benefit and are elderly or need extra heating for health reasons, you may be given help with heating costs (see page 77).

Is there anything you cannot claim?

1 If you get unemployment benefit, you cannot also claim sickness or invalidity benefits, retirement pension, maternity allowance or industrial injury benefit. If you qualify for any of these as well as unemployment benefit you will normally get paid whichever is higher.

2 You will not get the extra allowance for your wife if she earns more than £12·75 a week (£15·60 if you are sixty-five or over), or if she is getting a benefit such as a maternity allowance herself.

If you can't make ends meet

Which benefit?

1 If you have children and are working full time in a low-paid job, claim family income supplement. If you are married, or living as man and wife, it is the man who must have the job.
2 If you don't have a full-time job you may be able to get supplementary benefit, even if you have some earnings or savings.
3 If you are retired and not working full time, you may get a supplementary pension.
4 If you get supplementary benefit and have special needs (like a special diet prescribed by a doctor) you may get an exceptional circumstances addition. If you have a one-off need (like a heater or blankets) you may get an exceptional needs payment.
5 If your income is low, you may qualify for welfare benefits such as free prescriptions, help with dental or optical charges or free milk and vitamins for your children, even if you are not entitled to supplementary benefit or family income supplement.

Who gets it?

All these benefits are 'means tested'. This means that you need not have paid any NI contributions, but you will have to tell the social security office how much money you have and what your commitments are. If you get FIS or Supp. B. you will certainly be able to get all the welfare benefits; you may get them even if you don't get FIS or Supp. B.

How much is it?

These benefits depend on your income and the number of people you have to support. For example:

1 A family with two children and gross earnings of £58·50 (i.e., before taking off tax or National Insurance) would only get £7·75 FIS a week. If their earnings were £37 or less they would get the maximum of £18·50.

2 A family with two children under five years old, rent of £12 and an income of £36, might get £25 supplementary allowance. Even if they have no children, a couple whose income is £20 after paying rent might get £14 or so.

3 A retired couple whose income is £26 after paying the rent might get around £17·50 supplementary pension, as would a single OAP whose income after paying the rent is only £10.

4 Exceptional circumstances additions vary, but you might get up to £3·40 a week extra Supp. B. towards heating costs or £2·80 a week towards a special diet.

5 Welfare benefits include free NHS prescriptions, free or reduced cost dental treatment and dentures, glasses, free milk and vitamins for children under school age, and the refund of fares to and from hospital for treatment.

How do you claim?
1 For FIS, get leaflet FIS1 from a post office or social security office.

2 For a supplementary allowance, get form B1 from the unemployment office if you are unemployed; otherwise get leaflet SB1 from a post office or social security office.

3 For a supplementary pension use leaflet SB1.

4 For exceptional circumstances additions and needs payments you should ask at the social security office.

5 For welfare benefits get form M11 and for fares to hospital use form H11 from a post office, social security office or the hospital.

Can you get any other help?
If your income is low and you pay rent or rates you may be entitled to a rent and rate rebate (see page 53).

Is there anything you cannot claim?

1 You cannot have rent or rate rebates if you are getting Supp. B., because rent and rates are already allowed for in what you receive.

2 You can't get FIS if you are unemployed.

3 You can't have Supp. B. if you have a full-time job.

4 Your Supp. B. will be reduced by £12 a week if you are on strike – whether or not you get any strike pay from your union.

If you are ill

Which benefit?

1 You can get sickness benefit as soon as you have been off work for three days.

2 After six months' illness you can get an invalidity pension and, if you are under sixty (or fifty-five for women) an invalidity allowance as well.

3 If you started getting the invalidity pension after April 1979, you may be able to get an additional earnings-related pension on top, called an 'additional component'.

4 If you have not paid enough NI contributions to get the ordinary invalidity pension and allowance, you can claim a non-contributory invalidity pension after you have been ill continuously for twenty-eight weeks or more.

Who gets it?

1 The full benefits go to people who are normally employed or self-employed and paying Class 1 or 2 NI contributions. You can still get sickness and invalidity benefit even if you are over retirement age, provided you normally work.

2 If you are under retirement age but have not paid as many NI contributions as you should you can get the non-contributory invalidity pension after you have been ill continuously for twenty-eight weeks. Married women

who are too ill to go out to work or to do their normal housework can get this pension even if they have never paid any NI at all.

How much is it?
1 Sickness benefit is £20·65 for single people, or £33·40 if you qualify for an increase for a wife or other adult dependant. You also get an extra £1·25 for each child. Fred Simple, with his wife and two children, gets £35·90 a week.
2 Many people will get an earnings-related supplement as well, until it is phased out in January 1982. But you can't get the supplement if you are over retirement age – even if you were working before you became ill.
3 The invalidity pension is £26 a week, plus £15·60 for your wife or other dependent adult, and £7·50 for each child.
4 The invalidity allowance starts at £5·45 a week, which you will get if you were under forty when you became incapable of work. If you are forty to forty-nine you will get £3·45, and if you are fifty to fifty-nine (or fifty to fifty-four for women) you will get £1·15.
5 The non-contributory invalidity pension is £16·30 a week for single people, and £26·10 if you qualify for an increase for your wife or other adult dependant. You also get £7·50 for each child. So Fred Simple would get £41·10.

When is it paid?
1 Sickness benefit should start from the fourth day you are ill, so long as you claim promptly.
2 Invalidity benefit starts when you have been ill for twenty-eight weeks.

How do you claim?
1 For sickness benefit you must get a sick note from your doctor and send it to your local social security office

within six days of falling ill. Keep sending in sick notes for each week you are ill.

2 After twenty-eight weeks you should start getting invalidity pension, and allowance if you are young enough, without doing anything yourself.

3 For a non-contributory invalidity pension, use leaflet NI210 (or NI214 if you are a married woman) from your social security office.

Can you get any other help?

1 If there is no full-time wage coming in, you may get Supp. B. whether you have children or not (see page 144).

2 If your income is low you may get free dental treatment and dentures, glasses, prescriptions, milk and vitamins for the children.

3 If your income is low after paying rent or rates, you may be able to get rent or rate rebates (see page 53).

4 If you are disabled you may be able to get a mobility or attendance allowance. If you get an attendance allowance, then someone who looks after you may be able to get invalid care allowance (see page 150).

5 If you have to have hospital treatment as an out-patient, you may be able to get free travel to and from hospital. Get form H11 from the hospital or social security office, or if you get FIS or Supp. B., just take your order book to the hospital.

6 If you are on Supp. B. you may get help with heating costs.

Is there anything you cannot claim?

1 If you are getting sickness benefit or any invalidity pension you cannot qualify for unemployment benefit or a retirement pension, but if you qualify for any *other* benefit at the same time, you will normally receive a payment equal to the higher of the two you could get.

2 You cannot claim any sickness or invalidity pension or allowance if you earn more than a few pounds a week while ill.

3 You cannot claim any extra sickness benefit for your wife if she earns more than £12·75 a week. If she lives with you, then the extra you might get for her on your invalidity pension will be cut down if she earns over £45 a week or if she gets a benefit herself (such as the maternity allowance).

If you are disabled

Which benefit?
1 Attendance allowance.
2 Mobility allowance.
3 Invalid care allowance.

Who gets it?
1 The attendance allowance is a tax-free cash benefit for anyone over the age of two who is so physically or mentally disabled that they need to be looked after most of the time. The disabled person need not have paid NI, but he or she must have needed attention or supervision

for at least six months which can include time spent in hospital.

2 The mobility allowance is for anyone over five and under sixty-five when the allowance is claimed, who is so physically disabled that they can hardly walk. They need not have paid any NI, but it must be likely that they will be almost unable to walk for at least a year. Anyone who establishes their entitlement to the allowance before they are sixty-five can keep it until they reach seventy-five.

3 The invalid care allowance is for men and single women who have to stay at home to look after a relative who is getting either the attendance allowance or the constant attendance allowance under the industrial injuries or war pension schemes. You need not have paid any NI.

How much is it?
1 The attendance allowance is £21·65 for people who need to be looked after day **and** night; £14·45 for people who need to be looked after day *or* night.

2 The mobility allowance is £14·50 a week.

3 The invalid care allowance is £16·30 a week, plus £9·80 if you qualify for an increase for an adult dependant and £7·50 for each child. So if Fred Simple had to stay home to look after his wife, he would get £41·40. His wife would get an attendance or constant attendance allowance, and might qualify for a mobility allowance as well.

When is it paid?
1 The attendance allowance starts six months or more after you become disabled, or, for children, when they reach two years of age. Payment cannot be made for any time before the date of the claim, so claim promptly (see 1 below).

2 The mobility allowance can be claimed as soon as the disability starts, and can be paid from the date of the claim.

3 The invalid care allowance can start as soon as you claim, provided that an attendance allowance has been awarded.

How do you claim?
1 For the attendance allowance you should get leaflet NI205 from your social security office as soon as you, or the person you are looking after, have been ill for four months. If you are claiming for a child, get the form when they are twenty-two months, to give enough time for your claim to be processed and the payments to start as soon as possible.
2 For the mobility allowance use form NI211 as soon as you are disabled.
3 For the invalid care allowance, get leaflet NI212 from your social security office as soon as you think you can claim.

Can you get any other help?
1 If you were working when you became disabled, you can claim sickness benefit.
2 If you have children and are a full-time wage earner on a low wage, you may be entitled to FIS.
3 If there is no full-time wage coming in, you may get Supp. B. whether you have children or not.
4 If you were injured in war, you may get a war pension; write to: DHSS, North Fylde Central Office, Norcross, Blackpool FY5 3TA.
5 If your income is low and you pay rates or rent, you may get a rate or rent rebate.
6 If your income is low you may get welfare benefits such as free milk and vitamins for your children, free prescriptions, NHS glasses and dental treatment.
7 If you can work in spite of being disabled but find it hard to get there, you may be able to get three-quarters of the cost of a taxi – so long as you are registered disabled. Ask the disablement resettlement officer at your Jobcentre.

8 Children too disabled to go to school can get a free pint of milk a day – get form FW20 from your social security office.

9 If you are in need you may get extra Supp. B. to help with heating costs.

Is there anything you cannot claim?

1 You cannot get a mobility allowance if you are so ill in hospital that you cannot be moved.

2 You cannot normally get attendance allowance if you are getting constant attendance allowance under the industrial injuries or war pension schemes. However, if the constant attendance allowance is less than the attendance allowance, you will be paid the higher sum.

3 You cannot get invalid care allowance if you are already getting as much, or more, in other social security benefits. This is explained in leaflet NI212 from your local social security office.

If you are in hospital

If you, or someone you look after, goes into hospital, tell the social security office at once. Your benefits will be different.

1 If you get Supp. B. but have no family, you will only get £5·45 a week while you are in hospital. You will still get an allowance for any rent, rates, and so on, which still have to be paid. If you have a family and they need the Supp. B., they will still get it.

2 After four weeks in hospital your attendance allowance will stop.

3 If you are looking after someone who goes into hospital, your invalid care allowance will stop after four weeks – when their attendance allowance does.

4 After eight weeks in hospital, most other benefits will be

cut by £5·45 a week if you qualify as having a dependant, and by £10·90 a week if you do not.

5 After one year in hospital your benefits may be cut again. If you have no dependant, or do not choose to have the balance of your benefit paid to your dependant, you will get only £5·45 a week. The benefit you then do not get during your second year in hospital may be payable as resettlement benefit when you get better. You can choose to have all but £5·45 of your personal benefit paid to your dependant in the second year; but if you do this you will not get any resettlement benefit.

Save-it tip
Always tell the social security officer if anyone depends on you.

When you come out of hospital
If you have been in hospital for more than a year or so, ask about getting resettlement benefit as soon as you are dis-

If you have an accident at work you may get
industrial injury benefit.

charged. This will help you get back to normal life. Make sure you know all the other benefits you can get too, so you can stop worrying about money and concentrate on getting back on your feet.

If you get injured at work

Which benefit?
1 If you are injured you may get industrial injury benefit.
2 If your injury disables you, you may get industrial disablement benefit.

Who gets it?
1 If you have an accident at work, or contract certain illnesses because of the work you do, you may get industrial injury benefit. This does not depend on having paid a fixed number of NI contributions.
2 If you are disabled by an accident at work, or by an illness you get because of your work, you may be entitled to industrial disablement benefit. You need not be working in order to qualify.

How much is it?
1 Industrial injury benefit is £23·40 a week if you are on your own; £36·15 if you qualify for an increase for a wife or other adult dependant, and £1·25 for each child. If you still can't work after two weeks, are under pension age and have been paying full Class I NI, you may get an earnings-related supplement until the end of 1981. If you are under eighteen you will only get a lower flat rate although you may still get earnings-related supplement. Fred Simple, who was earning £80 a week before his accident, would start by getting £38·65. After two weeks he would also get an earnings-related supplement.
2 You will get more industrial disablement benefit the more

badly disabled you are. If you have lost a little finger you might get a lump sum of £1,000; for something worse you might get up to £2,950. If you are badly disabled you will get a weekly benefit rather than a lump sum. For example if you lost a hand you might get £26·80 a week; if you lost both hands, or your sight, you would get the maximum, which is £43·30 a week. You will get less if you are under eighteen.

When is it paid?
1 Industrial injury benefit can be paid for up to twenty-six weeks from the time of your accident (or the development of a listed occupational disease) if you are unable to work.
2 Industrial disablement benefit starts three days after your accident if you can still work, or when injury benefit stops if you can't work.

How do you claim?
1 To get industrial injury benefit you must report the accident to your employer at once. Then get a doctor's certificate (now called a 'statement') and send it to your social security office within six days. Get leaflet NI5 if you have had an accident, and NI2 if you have an occupational disease.
2 If you have been getting industrial injury benefit, you will be told about the possibility of getting disablement benefit when it stops. But if you are still working in spite of your disablement (and therefore not getting injury benefit), you should claim disablement benefit as soon as possible. Ask your social security office which form you need for your particular injury or illness.

Can you get any other help?
1 Receiving industrial disablement benefit will not affect any other NI benefits you may be getting, so long as you don't get the extra unemployability supplement. You may *also* get:

- a special hardship allowance of up to £17·70 a week if your disability means that you can't go back to as good a job as you had before;
- a constant attendance allowance of up to £17·70 a week if you need to be looked after all the time, or as much as £35·40 if you are very severely disabled indeed.
- an exceptionally severe disablement allowance if you get the higher rate constant attendance allowance and will always need to be looked after; this is £17·70 a week;
- a hospital treatment allowance, to bring your benefit up to £44·30 if you have hospital treatment;
- an unemployability supplement of £26 a week if you probably won't ever work again, plus an invalidity allowance such as you would get with an invalidity pension.

2 If you have children and there is a full-time but low wage coming in, you may get FIS (see page 201).

3 If your income is low and there is no full-time wage earner in the house, you may get Supp. B. (see page 144).

4 If you pay rates or rent you may get a rate or rent rebate (see page 53).

5 If your income is low you may be eligible for welfare benefits (see page 144).

6 If you qualify, you should apply for an attendance allowance, mobility allowance, or help with fares to work (see page 149).

7 If you are in need you may get extra Supp. B. to help with heating costs.

8 Anyone who looks after you every day or night may be able to get invalid care allowance (see page 149).

Is there anything you cannot claim?

1 If you get the unemployability supplement you cannot get special hardship allowance, unemployment, sickness, invalidity or widow's benefits, nor a retirement pension or other unemployability supplement or allowance.

156

2 You can't get any addition to the basic injury benefit if your wife earns more than £12·75 a week (£15·60 if you are sixty-five or over), or is receiving a personal benefit such as a maternity allowance.

If you are widowed

Which benefit?
1 Widow's allowance.
2 Widowed mother's allowance.
3 Widow's pension.
4 Industrial death benefits.
5 Death grant.

Who gets it?
1 You will get a widow's allowance if you are under sixty when your husband dies; if you are over sixty you will still get one so long as your husband was not entitled to a retirement pension when he died. Your husband must have paid NI at some time, but he need not have been working when he died.
2 You may get a widowed mother's allowance if you have a child under nineteen years old still living at home, and your husband paid enough NI contributions.
3 You will get a widow's pension if you are forty or over when your husband dies or when your widowed mother's allowance ends. Your husband must have paid enough NI to qualify.
4 You can get industrial death benefit if your husband dies as a result of an accident at work, or an industrial disease. It is paid instead of the widow's allowance, widowed mother's allowance or widow's pension.
5 You can get a death grant if your husband was born after July 1883, and either you or he paid NI.

How much is it?

1 The widow's allowance is £38 a week, plus £7·50 for each child, and you may get an earnings-related supplement depending on how much your husband earned. A woman with two children, whose husband earned £90 a week, gets £53 plus earnings related benefit until it is phased out in January 1982.

2 The widowed mother's allowance is £27·15, plus £7·50 for each child, and any extra pension your husband earned if he died after April 1979 (when the earnings-related scheme started).

3 The widow's pension is £27·15 a week if you are over fifty when your husband dies but it will be less if you are between forty and fifty. For example, if you are forty-five you will only get £17·65, and if you are forty you will only get £8·15. If your husband died after April 1979 you may get an additional pension as well.

4 Industrial death benefit is £38 a week for the first six months, plus £7·50 for each child, plus a supplement based on your husband's earnings. After six months you will get £23·85 plus £7·10 for each child; so if you have children you may be better off taking the widowed mother's allowance so long as you are entitled to any additional pension that your husband earned after April 1979. If you have no children and are under forty you only get £8·15.

5 The death grant is normally £30, but less for the very old and children.

When is it paid?

1 The widow's allowance is paid for the first six months after your husband dies.

2 The widowed mother's allowance and widow's pension are paid after the first six months are up, when the widow's allowance stops.

3 Industrial death benefit is paid from when you claim, and since you get less after the first six months you should claim as soon as you can.

How do you claim?

1 To get the widow's allowance, fill in the form on the back of the certificate you are given when you register your husband's death; take or send it to your social security office. You will then be sent another form, which you should fill in and return at once, or you may lose benefit.

2 The widow's pension or widowed mother's allowance should start automatically after you have been getting widow's allowance for six months. If this doesn't happen, ask why not.

3 To get industrial death benefit, you must fill in the special certificate given to you when you register your husband's death, and take or send it to your social security office.

4 To get the death grant, take or send the death certificate, your marriage certificate and any social security order books, together with the undertaker's estimate, to your social security office. You should do this as soon as possible, and always within six months of your husband's death. Don't worry if you haven't got all the papers; go and ask anyway.

Can you get any other help?

1 If you do not work full time you may get Supp. B.

2 If you are bringing up children on your own you may be able to get FIS even if you work only for twenty-four hours a week.

3 If your income is low you may get welfare benefits such as free prescriptions and NHS glasses even if you cannot get Supp. B. or FIS (see page 144).

4 If you pay rent or rates you may get a rent or rate rebate (see page 53).

5 If you are in need you may get extra Supp. B. to help with heating bills.

6 If your husband was killed in war, you may get a war widow's or dependant's pension; write to: DHSS, North Fylde Central Offices, Norcross, Blackpool.

Is there anything you cannot claim?

1 If you receive full-rate widow's benefit you cannot also claim any other benefit based on NI contributions, including: sickness, unemployment, maternity, invalidity or retirement benefits. But you *can* get any earnings-related supplement you would be entitled to along with these. And if you get a pension as an industrial injury or war widow, then any NI benefit you have earned by your own contributions will be paid on top of your pension.

2 You cannot get child benefit increase if you get a widowed mother's allowance, even if you are bringing up children on your own.

If you are retired

See Chapter 13.

If you have a family – or are starting one

See Chapter 12.

General hints on claiming

1 If you are not sure whether you or your husband have paid enough NI to get benefit, ask at your nearest social security office – which you can find under 'Health and Social Security, Dept of' in the phone book. It will help if you have your NI number, which your last employer will be able to tell you if you haven't any papers.

2 If your husband dies of an illness he contracted because of his work, check with the doctor exactly what he died from and ask your social security office for the right form.

3 If you can't get to a social security office to make your

claim, ask in the post office for a stamped, addressed envelope and send your claim in it.

4 If you are asked for papers such as your marriage certificate, try to find them. Only the social security staff will see them and your claim will be dealt with much more easily. Don't worry if you really can't find the papers; you can claim anyway.

5 If you are asked to go for a medical examination, don't be shy, go.

6 Always claim as soon as possible, or you may lose benefit.

7 If you don't know where your social security office is, ask in the post office or look in the phone book.

8 If you aren't sure about filling in the forms, ask at the social security office or a CAB.

Extra help from local authorities

The help offered varies; ask your local social services department at the town hall. You may have to pay something towards the cost, but the help is still worth it. For example:

- meals on wheels, or attendance at a day centre;
- help with the cost of a phone;
- cheap or free travel;
- holidays and outings;
- day centres;
- home nursing;
- visits from health visitors;
- wheelchairs, ramps, etc.;
- residential homes.

All you need to know about National Insurance

If you are between sixteen and pension age and earn £23 or more a week, you will have to pay NI. All the contributions go into a common fund out of which many of the social security benefits are paid. The main benefits paid out of the fund are:

- unemployment benefit;
- sickness benefit;
- retirement pension;
- widow's pensions and allowances;
- maternity grants and benefits.

If you work for an employer and earn a lot you will pay higher contributions, but to make up for this you will probably get an earnings-related supplement if you claim a benefit. If you don't pay enough NI you will not get the full rate of benefit, and may get nothing at all.

There are 4 classes of contribution. You pay:

- Class 1 if you work for an employer;
- Class 2 if you are self-employed;
- Class 3 if you have paid too little NI and want to catch up;
- Class 4 if you are self-employed and make more than £2,650 a year profit.

The benefits you can get depend on which sort of contributions have been paid.

If Class 1 have been paid, you can get the sickness, invalidity, unemployment, maternity and widow's benefits, retirement pension, child's special allowance and death grant.

If Class 2, or 2 and 4 have been paid, you can get the basic sickness, invalidity, maternity, and widow's benefits, basic retirement pension, child's special allowance and death grant. But you can't get unemployment benefit, so self-employed people should always make sure they have some savings and insurance of their own to fall back on.

If you have paid Class 3, you may have paid some Class 1 or 2 as well, and the combination may earn you some benefits. Your Class 3 contributions will help towards a maternity grant (but not the maternity allowance), widow's benefit, basic retirement pension, child's special allowance and death grant.

Paying Class 3 contributions will not help you get sickness, invalidity, or unemployment benefit; to be sure of these you must pay the full Class 1 or 2 contributions at the proper time. If you don't pay at the proper time you may lose benefit, so ask your social security office for advice before paying any Class 3 contributions to improve your record.

If you work for an employer

If you earn £23 or more a week you will pay Class 1 NI of 6¾p in every pound you earn, up to a maximum contribution of £11·14 if you earn £165 a week or more.

If you are over pension age you don't pay any NI, so you should get a certificate of age exemption from your social security office and give it to your employer. If you belong to your employer's pension scheme instead of the state's, you will pay a smaller NI contribution, but you may have to pay into the employer's occupational pension fund too. Your employer will do all the sums and take whatever is necessary from your wages – the amount will be shown on your pay slip.

If you work for more than one employer

If you earn £23 or more in each job you will have to pay Class 1 contributions for each job. But if you are already paying the maximum contribution in one job, you can apply to put off paying contributions in the other job by filling in the forms in leaflet NP28 from your social security office.

If you work for your husband or wife
You are an employee, so you have to pay Class 1 contributions if you earn £23 or more a week.

If you work through an agency
If you work regularly and are paid by the agency, they will take your NI from your wages before paying you. If they don't do this, ask them or your social security office how you should pay.

If you are self-employed
If you are self-employed you must pay Class 2 NI unless you get exemption – because of low earnings, for example. If your profit is more than £2,650 a year you will have to pay Class 4 as well. Class 2 stamps cost £2·50 a week. You can buy them at the post office each week and stick them on a card that you can get from your social security office; or you can pay through your bank or National Girobank by filling in the form in leaflet NI41, from your social security office. This is less trouble and you won't risk forgetting.

Class 4 contributions cost 5p in every pound profit between £2,650 and £8,300 a year. For example, Fred Pipe, a self-employed plumber, pays a £2·50 a week Class 2 contribution, but his profit is £5,000 a year, so he also pays 5p in every pound of his £2,350 excess profit. This makes £132·50 in Class 2 and £117·50 in Class 4, adding up to a total £250 a year. Your Class 4 NI will be collected by the income tax man.

If you expect to earn less than £1,250 profit a year you can ask to be excepted from paying any contributions at all – but remember that if you do this you may not get any benefits. Remember that if you are a company director, you must pay Class 1 contributions, even if you own the firm yourself.

If you are self-employed and work for an employer
You may have to pay Classes 1, 2 and 4 contributions. But

if you end up paying more than £415·50 a year you should ask for a refund of Class 4 contributions from the social security office. You should also ask for a refund if you pay more than £591·66 in Class 1 and 2 contributions in the tax year.

If you think you will end up paying more than these maximum amounts, you can apply to put off paying Class 2 or 4 contributions by filling in form CF359 in leaflet NP18, from your social security office.

If you are ill
If your employer goes on paying your wages, you will still have to pay Class 1 contributions. Otherwise, if you are off work for a whole week, you need not pay NI for that week. You will not lose any benefits as a result so long as you get a doctor's certificate and send it to your social security office explaining why.

If you are unemployed
If you are unemployed for a week or more, you need not pay NI so long as you register at your unemployment office.

If you are a married woman or a widow
If you are working you may be paying NI in the ordinary way, or you may be paying at a reduced rate. Which you do depends on whether you have the right to 'reduced liability'. This means that if you were married, or widowed and getting widow's benefit on 6 April 1977 and if you chose reduced liability by 11 May 1977, you should have had a certificate of election from your social security office. As a result, you will be paying a low rate NI contribution if you work for an employer, or no contribution at all if you are self-employed.

If you have reduced liability you can't get any benefits on your own insurance, but you may still get maternity grant, death grant or widow's benefit on your husband's. You will also qualify for a small retirement pension on his insurance when he retires.

If you are less than five years younger than your husband (or if you are older) it may be worth paying a full contribution. But if you are already widowed it will only be worth doing this if you are getting a reduced widow's pension or may remarry before you reach sixty. Remember, it will not be worth paying if you are nearing retiring age yourself, because you will not have time to pay enough contributions to earn a worthwhile pension.

Reduced liability is now being phased out, and if you stop work for two years on end you will lose your right to it and have to pay full contributions if you ever work again.

If you may decide to stop work in the future in order to bring up a family or look after an elderly or sick person, it may be worth paying full contributions now. If you do, you can qualify for home responsibilities protection which will improve your pension rights in the future.

Leaflets NI1 (if you are married) and NI51 (if you are widowed) explain the position in detail; but the choice is complicated and once you have opted to pay full contributions you can't go back to reduced liability. So if in any doubt, ask at your social security office.

If you are married for the first time, or following a divorce, after 5 April 1977, things are simpler – you have to pay full-rate contributions.

Widows who marry again after 5 April 1977 can keep their reduced liability if they had it as a widow.

If you are divorced

Even if you paid the reduced rate NI when you were married, you will now have to pay the full rate. You will have to tell your employer when your divorce comes through, so that he can change your contribution. You should also tell your social security office.

If you go on a training course
You may not have to pay NI; ask at your social security office.

General tips on paying NI

1 If you are over sixteen you should have a NI number – even if you aren't working. If you don't know it, ask your employer; if you've never had one, ask at your nearest social security office for a NI number card, and then keep it in a safe place.
2 If you miss paying some contributions, it may not be too late. Ask if you can pay them now.
3 Always tell your social security office if something happens that might change the contribution you should pay, for example: your husband dies, you get a second job, you remarry, you are ill or unemployed, or you get divorced.
4 If you don't know where your social security office is, look in the phone book under 'Health and Social Security, Dept of', or ask at the post office.
5 Remember that by not paying now you may lose benefits in the future.
6 Always check any queries with your local social security office. It is a very complicated area, and to get all the answers you may need far more detailed help than can be given here.

10 Home maintenance and improvement

Maintenance

Buying your own home is a good investment, and so is keeping it in good shape, for two reasons:

1 The house will be worth as much as possible.
2 It's less likely that you will need to call in builders, plumbers, and so on, to do expensive repairs. DIY will save a lot of money.

There are other ways of saving as well:

1 If you have a flood, turn off the water at the mains. Then try to mend things yourself, or get estimates from several plumbers. Never call a plumber at night or on Sundays if you can possibly avoid it. If there's nothing else to do, at least find out the total charge you will have to pay before the men arrive.
2 If there's a gas leak, call the gas board. They will turn off the mains for nothing and do a simple repair. Once things are safe you can take the time to find the best repair deal.
3 Always get three estimates for any repair or building job; look at each item as well as the total, or you may be asked to pay for extras like 'making good' which you had thought were included.
4 Check that estimates give a proper breakdown of where the money goes.
5 Do as many jobs as you can yourself, especially small ones. (Most firms have a minimum call-out charge, which makes small jobs very expensive.)

6 See if a neighbour will swap skills with you – you repair his car, he paints your front room.

7 Always try the simple solution before calling the experts. A new washer will cost a lot less than a plumber.

8 Be careful. Save money where you can, but don't take risks.

Home improvements

Many improvements will add to the value of your house, but not all. Find the ones that will and then remember that DIY saves money, and you may be able to get a grant towards the cost, too.

Which improvements are worth doing?

Before thinking about any individual improvements, it is worth remembering a few general rules:

1 Avoid things which are very much a matter of personal taste – they could make the house harder to sell.

2 Don't 'improve' beyond what is suitable to your house – people wanting to buy an ordinary three-bedroom semi are unlikely to want to pay extra for gold bath taps.

3 Remember that an improvement which costs you £200 to do today, might cost £400 to do in four years' time. Even if you only get back three-quarters of the value of the improvement if you sell then, you will still get £300; this is better than many investment schemes.

4 When it comes to any particular improvement, from building a garage to putting in central heating, you will want to ask yourself several questions before you go ahead:

- will it increase the value of my house?
- will it make my life more comfortable?
- will it make the house cheaper to run?

Possible improvements

Double glazing DIY systems can be quite cheap and easy to fit. The simplest are secondary windows which come as units with their own frames to fit inside yours. Most of the DIY systems will reduce the amount of heat you lose and make your house quieter and less draughty; but they won't add much to the value of the house.

Factory-made sealed units and replacement windows really need professional installation, and will cost you several hundred pounds. But they will cut your fuel bills by enough to recoup their cost in five or ten years and you should get back half what they cost to install when you sell the house.

For cheapness get DIY glazing, but if you can afford them install factory-sealed units, which will give you better insulation, better looks and increase the value of your house.

Roof insulation To cut fuel bills this is a must (see Chapter 5). It's unlikely to increase the value of the house, but if you haven't got it buyers may be put off. You may be able to get

a grant from your local authority to put it in; ask at the
town hall. It is very easy to insulate a roof, but always
remember to be careful with the glass fibre which can
irritate your hands and, far worse, your lungs.

Cavity wall insulation This is an expensive job and you
can't do it yourself. But it will increase the value of the
house, and save you its cost by lower fuel bills, in five years
or so. If you can afford it, and the rest of the house is already
well insulated, this would be a good step.

Garage A solid brick garage is a good investment for at
least three reasons: your car will last longer; you may well
pay less motor insurance; the value of your house will rise
by as much as the garage cost to build. A wooden garage
will help on the first count, but not much on the others.

Central heating It is hard to put in central heating yourself,
and it costs a lot to have installed professionally; but it will
certainly increase the value of the house, and, of course, in
most cases it will make you much more comfortable.
Dearest to install is probably oil – well over £1,000 for a
three-bedroom semi, and the running costs will not encourage
anyone to buy your house in the future.

Gas is next, at around £1,100, but you might add £750 or more to the value of your house.

Solid fuel will cost over £1,000, but probably adds £500 to the value.

Electric storage heaters are the cheapest of all to install, at perhaps £850 for four storage heaters, three panel heaters and an immersion heater – but the running costs should put off both you and future buyers of your house.

Think carefully before installing any sort of central heating, and calculate running costs (see Chapter 5), as well as the installation itself. The house will be more comfortable, but your fuel bills may be higher, and you certainly won't add the whole cost of installation to the value of the house. If you do go ahead, it is absolutely essential to have really good insulation – you will cut down the running costs and you should need a smaller, cheaper boiler too.

If you can't afford both, insulate rather than install central heating.

Fitted kitchen If you can do it yourself you should get back all you spend when you come to sell the house. To have it done professionally is nice, but a luxury that you can't bank on recouping the cost of.

Sliding patio-doors If you have a nice garden these should pay for themselves when you sell. Remember that big panes must be double glazed. The cost varies a lot, so shop around; you could pay between £250 and £600.

Extensions A well-built extension that adds a good-sized room and looks right with the rest of the house will always pay for itself when you sell, and if the house was very small you may even make a profit. If you can build it yourself, you are even more likely to increase the value of the house by more than the extension cost. Remember: you may need planning permission – ask at the town hall before you start.

Showers A separate shower off the main bedroom will increase the value of the house; an electric shower over the bath probably won't – but you may save on fuel (see Chapter 5).

Separate lavatory If you can find room for a separate and second lavatory, it will add value; dividing the bathroom probably won't. If there is no indoor lavatory at all you can get a grant to install one; ask at the town hall.

Built-in wardrobes Do it yourself, and you will increase the value of the house by the cost of the materials, or more if you get them cheaply – so shop around.

Making a through lounge If you have two small rooms and two or more other bedrooms, knocking down the wall will almost always add to the value of the house. You can do it yourself, but always check the ceiling support first, and don't go ahead unless you're sure it is strong enough. If you have two reasonably sized rooms it's better to leave them separate.

Loft conversion This is well worthwhile if you can make a proper room and fit in stairs without ruining the room below; you should recoup the cost when you sell. If you can't do it properly it's better not to do it at all; at least if you want a financial return. Again, check whether you need planning permission before you start.

Porches These won't add value to the house – in fact, buyers may not like them.

Sheds and greenhouses These may make the house more attractive when you sell, but probably won't actually increase its value.

Which jobs are worth doing yourself?
If you are thinking of adding any of the 'value adding' improvements, you will obviously have an even better investment if you spend less in the first place by doing it yourself. You can save a lot by doing your own maintenance and repair jobs too. But don't start on any improvements or maintenance jobs unless you are sure you can complete them – getting someone to sort out the mess will cost as much, if not more, than having the professionals from the start.

Some DIY jobs are far more worthwhile than others; apart from saving on labour costs you will save even more if you buy second hand from breakers' yards and junk shops, design carefully to avoid the wastage that builders just add on to the bill, buy all the materials in discount stores. The biggest savings will probably come from:

- car servicing and repairs;
- repairing domestic appliances;
- building home extensions and garages (but it's hard work and needs equipment that will add a lot to the cost unless you can borrow it);
- installing central heating (but it's quite difficult);
- electric wiring (but always make sure you know what you're doing);
- carpentry (the more complicated the job, the more you save);
- outside painting;
- loft insulation.

Grants for home improvements
Improvement grants These are given by local authorities for various structural improvements such as damp proofing, and for repair costs, up to an equivalent amount as improvements, done at the same time. The authority decides who to give grants to and they are normally for real improvements in living conditions, rather than in the look of the house.

You can apply for an improvement grant if the rateable value of your house is less than £225 (£400 in London).

If you get a grant, it will usually be for half the total cost of the work, although if you live in a Housing Action or General Improvement Area you may get up to 90 per cent. You won't get anything towards costs over £5,000, so in most cases the biggest grant you can hope to get is £2,500.

Intermediate grants If you don't have a bath, indoor lavatory or hot and cold running water, you can get an intermediate grant to put them in. In most cases you have a right to these grants, and you should apply to the local authority. Again, you will normally get half the cost of the work, but nothing towards any costs over £2,700. Repairs can be covered as well.

Mrs. J wrote in to *Money-Go-Round* to ask if she could get any help with putting an indoor lavatory in her terrace house in Lancashire. Six months later, in January, she wrote to us again to tell us that the council had given her the money and 'I've never had such a happy Christmas, not having to worry about the children going down the garden in the cold.'

Repair grants If you live in a Housing Action or General Improvement Area you may be able to get a grant towards repairs costing up to £1,500 that you couldn't afford to do yourself. The local authority decides who gets them and what for, but the most likely cases are those where health could be affected, such as getting rid of damp or condensation. Ask at the town hall if you have this sort of problem.

Special grants If you share your house with another family you may be able to get a grant towards putting in extra bathrooms, lavatories, basins, hot and cold water, and so on.

Insulation grants If you haven't got any roof insulation, and your hot-water tank isn't lagged, you can get money to help pay to put things right. If you own your own home, are a landlord, or rent from a private landlord, you may get up to £60, or two-thirds of the cost, whichever is less. For example, if the insulation cost £100 you would get £60; but if it only cost £60, you would only get £40. The grants are only for insulating lofts and tanks, and you can't get one if you already have loft insulation (however bad), nor just for lagging tanks and pipes.

The rules are rather different in Scotland, but grants are still available; ask your local authority.

11 Transport and holidays

You probably spend 10p in every pound you earn just on getting around; you will only spend more on the roof over your head and the food you eat. Does it really have to cost so much?

The real cost of running a car

Public transport costs are rising, but a car is still usually even more expensive. There is a lot more to running a car than just petrol.

Depreciation
If you buy a new car for £3,000, you might get only £2,000 for it two years later. Two years after that you might only get £1,500 – so in just four years you have spent £1,500, or over £1 a day, without driving an inch. Worse still, if you want to replace the car you sell, it will cost you a lot more than the £3,000 you had to spend four years ago. Older cars lose their value less quickly, but they may cost more in other ways, like repairs and petrol consumption.

Interest
If you had put the money you spend on buying a car in the building society instead, it would have earned interest. Even a deposit of £600 for a car on HP would earn around £1 a week and if you then invested all the instalments you would easily earn over £150 a year.

Tax and insurance
The law demands a vehicle excise licence costing £60 a year, and insurance that will hardly cost less than £60 even if you only have third party, unless you have a big no-claims discount (see page 139). For a comprehensive policy, you will probably start at £150 a year.

Repairs and maintenance
If you can do your own repairs and maintenance you will save labour costs, which are currently around £8 an hour. If you have to use a garage your bill could easily run to over £300 a year, but if you do all the work yourself you should be able to halve it.

Petrol
At £1·30 a gallon, doing the average 33 mpg for 100 miles a week will cost £3·94 a week, or £204·88 a year.

Extras
Oil, tyres, batteries and parking fees will add at least £25 a year, even if you only drive a fairly modest 5,000 miles.

The grand total
Bill Simple buys a one-year-old car for £2,400. He only drives 10,000 miles a year and does most of his own maintenance; he has the maximum no-claims discount on his comprehensive policy. Even so, the car costs him:

depreciation	£380
lost interest	£100
tax	£ 60
insurance	£ 60
repairs	£282
petrol	£366
extras (including membership of a motoring organization)	£ 51
TOTAL	£1,299

178

Bill Simple is a perfect motorist, yet his driving costs him nearly 13p a mile; most of us would spend more!

Do you really need a car?

If you live in town and use the car only for occasional trips and your annual holiday, going by taxi or hiring a car would be cheaper than owning one. At £2 or £3 a day before you start driving at all, a car is a luxury. It could be more convenient not to own a car too; you will certainly have fewer parking or breakdown worries.

If you live in the country, have a young family, regularly go on longish trips, or have to drive to work, a car may be a necessity. It will make more economic sense too, because the fixed charges like insurance and tax will be spread over more miles. Even so, you can save a lot by buying wisely and driving carefully.

Cutting the costs

Buying   Buy the smallest car you can manage with; they use less petrol and cost less to insure.

Don't buy a sports car, especially if you are young and new to driving; the insurance will be much higher.

Don't buy unusual foreign makes, which tend to depreciate quickly and may be hard to get repaired.

.Get a proper guarantee from a dealer, for a reasonable time and covering all spares. Consider a warranty from one of the motoring organizations, to cover mechanical breakdowns.

Check that the dealer belongs to one of the trade organizations (Motor Agents' Association, Scottish Motor Trades Association, Society of Motor Manufacturers and Traders). Then if things do go wrong, there is a code of practice for handling complaints.

If you buy privately, you won't get a guarantee, so it is very important to get the car checked by the AA or RAC unless you really are an expert. At £22 to £35, it is money well spent, even if you have to join the organization, which will cost you another £15 but brings lots of other help with travel, insurance and legal advice, technical advice and free roadside assistance if you break down.

With new cars, check exactly what is included in the price, since delivery, number plates, seat belts, and so on, may be extra.

Private deals can be the sources of second-hand bargains, but traders in second-hand cars know far too much to let a good car go too cheap. You should beware of all apparent bargains, there may be a catch, but you may get a good deal in the autumn when many people trade in their cars in order to get a new one with the new registration letter.

Never buy in a car auction unless you know a lot about cars; you probably won't be able to have a test drive and you won't get any guarantee.

Depreciation Second-hand cars are cheaper to buy and lose their value less quickly, but they are more likely to need repairs. After three years or so, the increase in repair costs is likely to outweigh the decrease in depreciation, so unless you are a good mechanic don't buy a car over three years old.

Insurance Earn a no-claims discount, and don't claim for damage that will cost less to put right than your discount is worth, unless your policy gives you a protected no-claims discount.

Get the right insurance. For old bangers, third party, fire and theft will do; but for newer cars you need comprehensive (see page 138). It is worth shopping around, but always read the policies carefully to check they cover all you want.

Repairs and maintenance Do your own, or get a mechanically-minded friend to do them for you and paint his kitchen or dig his garden in return.

Avoid rare foreign cars where spares may be hard to get.

Service your car regularly rather than wait for it to break down.

Don't over-rev the engine or slip the clutch.

Petrol Don't buy a higher octane than the car needs; it's a waste of money. Don't buy a lower octane than is recommended for your car though – you will damage the engine.

Check that the gauge reads zero before your tank is filled; watch how much petrol you get and check the bill.

Drive smoothly, in the highest gear you can.

Extras Make sure you pass the MOT first time; each retest costs £2·80.

Keep tyres at the right pressures and don't scrape the kerb when you park.

Avoid fines; keep to the speed limit (which will save petrol, too), and only park where you are allowed to.

Travelling by bus

Buses are often cheaper than trains, especially for longer trips, so compare the costs every time. You can probably save money by getting a season ticket if you do the same trip regularly on country buses. In many places retired people can get passes or tokens and then travel cheaply, or even free, within the area; so if you are retired, or know someone who is, ask at the town hall about special fare schemes. Young people can save money too; remember: children under five may go free and school children at half-price.

Travelling by train

If you travel every day by train you should certainly get a season ticket. The longer the period you can get it for, the better, since the savings are greater and you may avoid a fare increase for a while. Even if you take a month's holiday, an annual season ticket will cost less than eleven monthly ones, so ask your employer if he will lend you the money (see pages 11 and 41) or use a bank budget account.

For family trips you might save money with a family Railcard. It will cost you £16, but then you can take another adult and up to four children on a trip for only 50p each, while you pay the ordinary fare. Unless you are only travelling a few miles it will certainly be worth having one of these cards. There are special Railcards for senior citizens too. You can buy a card for £8, which entitles you to half-price day-return, ordinary single or return tickets. Again, unless you only travel a few miles a Railcard will save you money – and it is valid for a whole year.

For students and school children over fourteen, a student Railcard can be a very good buy. They cost £8 for a year, and allow you to pay half-price for ordinary and day-return tickets.

For holidays, ask about monthly return fares, and special excursion tickets. Even if you are not a student, nor an OAP, and you don't want to take the children, you can still save a bit if you buy the right sort of ticket. Big City Savers, between London and many big cities, cost around half the ordinary return fare, but you must book at least a day before you travel. 'Awayday' returns cost a little more, and they are only for day trips, but weekend and monthly returns will save a bit on longer journeys. Train fares are high, so it is worth finding the cheapest sort of ticket and maybe going outside the rush-hour, during which cheap tickets may not be available.

Travelling by coach

Coaches run between many big cities and cost about half the second-class rail fare. They do take longer, and many people find them less comfortable, but if you want to save money, it will be worth the inconvenience.

Travelling by air

This can be a very expensive way of getting around within the UK, but fares are now being cut by large amounts – and it is fast. Although the number of routes on which there are stand-by flights is limited, it should be cheaper than having a seat booked; but if speed is what you're after you can't risk getting left behind. Travelling abroad by air is quite a different thing because package trips have slashed the cost – see the next section.

Going on holiday

Holidays are no fun if you feel you will need to do overtime for the rest of the year to pay the bill, so how can you find the cheapest way of enjoying yourself most?

Staying at home
About a third of us do not go away for our holidays at all. If money is tight it will be best to stay at home, but go on trips to local places, eat different food, or simply lie in bed in the morning. Indulge yourself just a bit and you can have a good holiday without moving out of your own home town.

Staying in the UK Most of us spend our holidays in the UK, and half the time we stay with friends or relatives, which, of course, is cheap. Staying in hotels in the UK could cost as much as going abroad on a package tour, so don't always assume you can save money by not crossing the Channel.

Camping Many campsites only cost a few pounds a week, and a farmer may let you camp free in his field for the odd night. You could camp free on common land, but do make absolutely sure it is common before you pitch your tent. It is

sensible to borrow a tent until you are sure you'll like camping, or go to a site where tents are provided; even with washing facilities as well this should only cost £20 a week for four people. Most campers travel under their own steam, but if you do not, remember to check for cheap rail or coach fares.

Caravanning If you have a car the travel cost will be quite low, but check that your insurance policy is still valid when you are towing a caravan, or whether you need to pay an extra premium. Sites only cost around £10 to £15 a fortnight, depending on where they are and the facilities provided. Hiring a caravan will, of course, cost more, maybe £40 a week or so, but it is a good idea the first time, and then if you like it, a caravan will be a good investment.

Holiday camps A self-catering chalet for four might cost £60 to £120 a week in mid-summer, but out of season the cost could be as low as £40. Check how much extra you would pay for all your meals, and compare it with your own cooking costs; you may not save a lot by doing it yourself. You should also ask when the off-season rates start, since you might save a lot by taking your holiday just out of the busiest time. Always make sure you know exactly what is included in the price by way of entertainments or facilities like baby-sitting; it could be a nasty shock to find you had to pay extra.

Hotels You are unlikely to pay less than £50 a week per person, just for bed and breakfast. So how can you keep the price as low as possible? Always ask about reductions for children, and check exactly what extras, such as entertainment, are included in the price. You will often pay less by choosing one of the packages which many hotel chains run and which any travel agent should be able to tell you about. If you just want bed and breakfast, a guest house or farm might suit you well, and could cost as little as £25 per week per person.

Remember that if you have to cancel a booking you should always give as much notice as you can. If you just don't turn up, you could have to pay almost the whole bill.

Going abroad
Going abroad need not cost more overall than staying in the UK, but the money is different, and different things cost more, so it's easy to spend more than you meant to. To avoid this, ask your travel agent, friends and the country's tourist office a few questions:

How much does food cost in shops and restaurants, and which foods are cheap and which dear? If you're cooking for yourself it could be worth taking some of the things that cost far more with you.

How much do different drinks cost? It is always cheaper to drink what the locals drink, so it helps to go to places where you like the local tipple.

Is your hotel on the beach and near shops, or will you need to take buses and taxis? If you will need transport, ask how much it will cost.

What sort of clothes will you need? Buying clothes in holiday resorts can be very expensive.

Will you need medical insurance (see page 191)?

Where to go   Most countries cost a bit more to live in than the UK, but Italy, Gibraltar, Spain, Turkey, Greece and Yugoslavia are less expensive than elsewhere. For a cheap holiday you should probably avoid France, Germany, Holland, Scandinavia, Austria and Belgium unless, of course, you will be staying with friends. Going outside Europe can be very expensive, but there are cheap fares and packages to be had.

Where to stay   Apart from going on a package holiday, the cheapest way is to camp or take a caravan. Remember, however, that while you won't have a big hotel bill, petrol can cost a great deal, and you will need insurance in case anything goes wrong. If you do decide to stay in a hotel you should allow at least £10 a night per person.

Driving abroad Always check the cost of petrol and the octane levels available in all the countries you will visit, and make sure you take advantage of the cut prices available to tourists in Italy, Greece and several eastern European countries. Even if you have these, calculate your mileage carefully and don't go further than you need. Three thousand miles could cost well over £100 in petrol, and won't help by being on the clock when you sell. Remember also that you have to pay to use a lot of the motorways in Europe. The French *autoroutes* are particularly expensive, and the bill for towing a caravan from Calais to the South of France would be well over £50. Crossing the Channel with a car, two adults and two children will add another £50 or so.

Caravanning Sites can cost £70 for two weeks, or well over £80 if you want to hire a caravan. For that price many offer good facilities, so make sure yours does before you go. Last summer the *Money-Go-Round* team dealt with a heap of letters about the sorry state of some foreign caravan sites. Mr B from Nottingham was so disgusted that 'I took my family away to a hotel the next morning; it cost a lot, but that place was awful.' If you take your own caravan you will have fewer worries, but you will pay £30 or more to cross the Channel, and use more petrol.

Flying abroad
Wherever you go there will be lots of different prices, even on the same flight. So ask your travel agent which will be cheapest for you, and always ask some time before you want to go. You can usually get a cheaper fare if:

– you book several weeks or months ahead;
– you stay at least one week and usually not more than a month in Europe. Overseas destinations usually have longer maximum stays;

- you don't book at all. Check whether last minute stand-by seats are offered on your route and decide whether the saving is worth the risk (this isn't wise in the high season, but at less popular times of the year it can be);
- you take advantage of cheap fares for young people over two and under twelve, and in some cases youth or student fares are available to those in their teens or early twenties;
- you travel out of the main season;
- you travel on a weekday, at night;
- you travel on an airline that has special prices for families travelling together.

Charter flights   These are advertised in lots of magazines and newspapers, and they can be cheap, but you can lose your money if you are not careful. So, check that the tour operator has an ATOL number, and is a member of ABTA (The Association of British Travel Agents); then if you have a complaint there is a code of practice to help sort it out, an independent arbitration scheme to decide who is in the right, and funds to compensate you for any money you may have lost. More important, perhaps, by sticking to the reputable, registered operators, you are less likely to have anything go wrong in the first place.

Package holidays   This is usually the cheapest way of going abroad, and there are packages to suit all tastes and pockets. You shouldn't have any money worries, but it is best to check:

1 The rules on cancelling; you may have to pay the full cost of the holiday if you cancel less than six weeks before your departure. If it is at all likely that you may have to cancel, insure against it.
2 When you have to pay the bill; it may be six weeks before you go, so start saving early.
3 That you are getting the best deal; different companies may offer the same holiday at different prices.
4 What is included in the price; meals, excursions or enter-

tainments may be extra, as may travel from the airport to your hotel.

5 That there won't be a last-minute surcharge if the value of the pound falls; several firms now guarantee not to put on this sort of surcharge, and ABTA members can't make currency surcharges less than thirty days before you leave.

6 That the firm is a member of ABTA so that if anything goes wrong you will have the best possible chance of sorting it out.

7 That if there's any possibility of a fuel surcharge, the terms are fully explained.

Taking your money abroad

Be realistic about how much money you will need. Running out of cash abroad is no fun, and it is much better to bring some back unspent. Think what you will need to buy – meals, fares, and so on – and how much extra you can afford for drinks, ice-creams and presents. Add a bit more for emergencies, which you will try not to spend. When you get there, try to stick to what you worked out, with an allowance for each day. It is a good idea to note down what you spend, otherwise, with unfamiliar money, it is very easy to lose track completely.

Cash   Take £20 worth in the currency of each country you will visit, to cover anything you may need as soon as you arrive, when the banks may not be open. It is risky to take more than this, because if you lose cash it is gone forever. Any bank in this country will sell you foreign money, even if you don't have an account; but you should ask a week before you need it, or longer if you are going somewhere unusual.

Travellers' cheques   Any bank and some travel agents will sell you these. They are safe because no one except you can use them, unless they forge your signature. You can prevent even this danger by sending a telegram to your bank if you lose your cheques; it will then refuse to pay out on any more of them. It is best to get travellers' cheques in the currency of the country you are going to, particularly if you are visiting the USA, but if you are going to several different countries you could take pound or dollar cheques that you can change wherever you go. If you take pound cheques you should try to cash them in a bank, rather than a shop or hotel where you will probably get less for them. Always take your passport when you go to cash a cheque, and don't sign it till you get to the cashier.

Remember to keep a note of all your cheque numbers, separate from the cheque book, so that if you lose the cheque book you can tell your bank all the details.

Ordinary cheques If you have a bank account and a cheque card with the Eurocard symbol on it, you can get £50 a day at any bank abroad which shows the symbol. This is useful for emergencies, but the foreign bank may charge a fee, so it is best only to get cash in this way if you have to.

Credit cards You can't use credit cards to get cash abroad, but you can pay the bill at restaurants, hotels, garages, and so on, where the signs are displayed. However, don't rely on being able to use credit cards everywhere, because you may find they aren't accepted just when you need the money most; and try not to use them at all unless you know you are getting a reasonable exchange rate.

If you run out of cash If you have a bank account at home you can send a telegram, asking for money to be sent to you, giving the exact name and address of a local bank where the money can be sent. As a last resort you can contact the nearest British Consulate. They will *lend* you enough money to get home, but you will always have to pay it back, and this really is something for emergencies only.

Insurance for your holidays

Things do, sadly, go wrong on holiday. But at least if you have proper insurance a mishap will not turn into a disaster. There are many good package insurance schemes that will cover you for illness, losing your money or luggage and all the other likely accidents.

In case you are ill We are used to getting free medical treatment on the NHS, but different systems operate abroad. In Common Market countries you may be asked to pay a doctor on the spot; but if you fill in form E111 (obtainable from most post offices) before you leave this country you will be able to get back most of the cost of medical treatment when you arrive home. However, it is still sensible to have insurance as well because it will cover things like getting the patient home, staying longer than you had intended, extra travel costs and fees you may have to pay if illness makes you cancel the holiday before you go. A good package policy to cover these things should only cost around £6 for two weeks in Europe, which is money very well spent. Outside the Common Market insurance is a must. In the USA and Canada doctors' fees can be very high, and you will need medical insurance of at least £5,000. Policies are available for up to £20,000, which could cost you £25 for two weeks, and it is important to have this proper cover. It is also particularly important to get medical insurance if you are going on a ski-ing or mountaineering holiday where accidents are more likely to happen. It will probably cost two or three times as much as insurance for any other holiday, but you should certainly buy it nevertheless. With package holidays, package insurance is sometimes included. If so, check what is covered, and for how much, because you may want more, particularly if you are going outside Europe. You might get a better policy from the travel agent, separate from your tour operator's package deal; so always check that you're getting the best deal, and if you don't want the package insurance, be sure to cancel it.

Your car First ask your car insurers whether your ordinary policy will cover the legal requirements in the countries you are going to. Tell them where you are going and whether you will be taking a caravan. Most policies should cover the legal minimum you must have, but you may not have such good cover as your policy gives you at home. Accidents and breakdowns abroad can also be far more expensive than they would be at home because of extra transport or hotel costs, so you should get extra insurance. Both the Automobile Association and the Royal Automobile Club have policies to cover emergency repairs, towing to a garage, extra fares, hotel expenses that you have to pay while you wait for your car to be repaired, and so on. At a cost of around £15 for four weeks, this is well worth it.

Luggage Losing your luggage is not so bad as an accident, but it is a nuisance and expensive. A standard holiday insurance policy will cover this, as well as illness, but always check exactly what is covered, for how much and where. You don't want to lose something only to be told that that sort of loss wasn't included in your policy.

Before you leave

1 Get things organized at least three weeks before you go; forms and policies can take a long time to be processed.
2 Get your insurance when you book the holiday, so that you will be covered if you have to cancel.
3 Check the application form to see that all the countries you are visiting are included, and all the risks you want to cover are covered – suitcases in hotel rooms, money in the car, accidents on boats or whatever you may feel is important. If the insurance is part of a package holiday, ask to see the policy certificate itself, not just a description of it; and if you don't understand it ask the travel agent to explain.
4 If you are elderly, or travelling with elderly people, make sure there isn't an age limit on who the insurance includes.
5 If any of the party is ill or pregnant when you book your

holiday, tell the insurance company and check that the policy doesn't exclude them. If you don't tell them, and then want to make a claim, they needn't pay; if you do tell them, they may restrict the cover or possibly even turn you down, but at least you'll know where you stand.

6 Store the policy certificate carefully, and take a copy with you, then if the policy gets lost you will still be able to make a claim when you return if you need to.

7 Get a policy that covers you for delays in departure; so if you are unlucky enough to be stuck in an airport for days, you will at least get some compensation.

When things go wrong

1 Report any accident or theft to the hotel and local police at once. If you are in an airport or station tell the official staff. If you are on a package tour tell the tour representative. Ask the person you tell to confirm *in writing* that you did so; the insurance company, the police or a lawyer may want to check later on.

2 Make sure you get, and keep, any bills from doctors, garages or hotels, so that you will be able to prove that your claim is correct.

3 Inform the insurance company immediately on your return.

12 Families and children

When couples first get married they are usually both working, so there are two wage packets to live on. When children arrive there will probably only be one wage packet to feed more people. Of course most families get by somehow or another, but a lot of the worries could be avoided by planning, and knowing what to do in certain situations.

Planning

It is sensible to put off having children until one parent is earning enough to support the whole family, unless you are certain you can find proper day care and both want to go on working. Family planning is free on the NHS, so this shouldn't be hard. If you do have an unplanned baby, you will almost certainly manage, and love it just as much as any other; but you may have to be more careful and tighten your belt a bit more than if you had waited. If you really don't think you can cope – if you have lots of children already or are on your own perhaps, go to your GP as soon as you know you are pregnant and ask his advice; or get in touch with the British Pregnancy Advisory Service or other charities that will help and can arrange safe abortions free or at very little cost.

Budgeting

Budgeting is always important, especially with a family, and even more so if the family arrived before time. Have another look at Chapter 3 for how to manage your basic budget, then you will have to make some changes because of the children. The main changes are:

1 A mother – or father – may stop working, but will still need a bit of money to spend just as she – or he – pleases.
2 You will probably use more fuel because babies need to be warm, there will be people in the house more of the time, and there will be more washing.
3 With more time at home you may be able to spend more time cooking and cut down on expensive quick meals. But it's no good buying cheap cuts of meat only to run up big fuel bills because they need longer cooking. Remember to use the oven economically (see page 82).
4 At first babies take up very little room, but they soon grow. If your home will be too small for a toddler, you should start saving for a bigger home before it comes urgent.

The cost of having a baby

Medical care This is more important than anything, and it is free. You won't have to pay for prescriptions or dental treatment, let alone a doctor or hospital, while you are pregnant or with a small baby. Take advantage of this; go to all the classes, and check-ups, you are offered, and see the dentist.

Private treatment could cost hundreds of pounds and is rarely covered by insurance.

Clothes for you You will save a lot if you borrow, swap and alter clothes wherever you can; but you should reckon to spend £50 even so.

Clothes for the baby Just buying the absolute minimum could easily cost you £50. People are very generous to babies, though, and if you can persuade friends to give you nappies,

195

stretch suits, and so on, rather than too many white matinée jackets, you will save a lot of money and your baby will be just as happy. He won't notice if clothes are new or not, so borrow, swap or buy second-hand where you can. Remember that babies grow very fast, so long-lasting new clothes are really a waste of money; and because babies grow so fast there is also no point in getting too many clothes in the smallest sizes.

Baby equipment Tiny babies may need less in the way of expensive equipment than the adverts would have you believe, but there are some things that they really do need. Talk to other mothers about what they found most useful, and then work out which things your particular baby will need. Remember:

- a big pram will be worse than useless if you have a flight of steps up to the front door or nowhere to keep it;
- the kitchen sink can do as a baby bath till you can put the baby in the proper bath (but make sure the taps can't burn him);
- a carry-cot with wheels can do as both pram and cradle for the first few months, then you can move on to a pushchair and cot without ever needing a pram or crib;
- fitted bottom sheets may make your life easier, but you can simply cut up any spare sheets of your own (it's not a good idea to use nylon, but flannelette or cotton will be fine);
- breast feeding is cheaper, as well as better, for the baby, so try it and keep it up if you possibly can;
- keep your eyes open for second-hand baby things in local papers, newsagents or from friends and neighbours.

What help can you get?
The maternity grant If you or your husband have been working for an employer or been self-employed and you have paid your NI contributions, you will almost certainly get

the grant of £25. Get a claim form from your GP, maternity clinic or social security office from fourteen weeks before, to three months after the baby arrives. Single mothers can get the grant if they have paid enough NI contributions themselves. If you and your husband have both been out of work for some time you should ask the social security office if you can still get the grant; it is always worth asking.

The maternity allowance This is a weekly allowance of £20·65 plus an earnings-related supplement until January 1982. You may also get £1·25 for each child you have, including the new one, if you are an unsupported mother. Maternity allowance is paid for eighteen weeks, starting the eleventh week before the baby is due. You will only get the allowance if *you* have paid NI; your husband's contributions don't count; and you can't get the allowance while you are working, although it won't be cut if you get maternity pay from your employer. If you are already a single parent, you should get the £3 child benefit increase for your first child, instead of the £1·25 addition to your maternity allowance.

Get a claim form from your GP, maternity clinic or social security office fourteen weeks before your baby is due – it is the same as the grant form. Remember that if you claim less than eleven weeks before the baby is born you may lose some benefit because the maternity allowance will not be backdated.

Free milk and vitamins If you get FIS or Supp. B., you will get free milk and vitamins while you are pregnant, and so will any other children you have under school age.

Free dental treatment If you are pregnant or have a baby under a year old, you can get free dental treatment and dentures.

Free prescriptions If you are pregnant or have a baby under a year old you should get an exemption certificate so that you do not have to pay for prescriptions. If you are pregnant, your doctor, midwife or health visitor will give you a form to fill in and send to the Family Practitioner Committee. If you fail to do this, you can still get exemption after the baby is born by filling in form FP91 available from post offices and social security offices.

If you find it hard to make ends meet it is worth asking at your social security office whether you can get these welfare benefits even if you don't fit into either of the groups that get them automatically.

What if you want to go back to work? If you go back to work after the baby is born, you will have to pay someone else to look after it. This may make it hardly worth while from the money angle, depending on how much you can earn, but you may want to go back to work so as to carry on with your career. If you know before the baby is born that you will want to go back to work, you will be able to keep your job and get paid maternity leave from your employer if:

- you have been working for the same employer for at least two years;
- you go on working till eleven weeks before the baby is due;
- you tell your employer at least three weeks before you leave that you want your job back.

He will then have to keep your job for you for twenty-nine weeks after the baby is born, and he will have to pay you 90p in every pound of your normal salary for six weeks. He will take the flat rate £20·65 of your state maternity benefit off what he gives you, even if you don't in fact qualify for it; but you will still almost certainly be better off than if you had given up work completely.

The cost of children from 0–16

All children need food, clothes, warmth, amusements and interests, but they need not cost a fortune. Expensive toys, outings, holidays, and so on, may be fun, but they are not so important as a loving home where children are encouraged to find ways – cheap if need be – of amusing and interesting themselves in worthwhile pursuits.

From birth to 5 years
You should allow an average of perhaps £5 a week for food, and £2 for clothes and extras. A tiny baby will cost less, especially if it is breast fed, but a toddler will need this much. Beds, prams, and so forth, are easy to find second-hand, and you can sell them again when you no longer need them. Extras like toys, sweets and trips can cost as much as you like; but although a few are nice, don't worry if you can't afford many – a toddler can be as well amused by a saucepan and a wooden spoon as by an expensive toy. You may need extra heating, and you should check with your GP or health visitor if you are unsure whether the baby's room is warm enough. If you are in serious difficulty over paying for the heating you need, and you are getting Supp. B., ask at your local social security office if you can get extra help.

From 5–11 years
Food need still only cost £5 a week or so if you are careful, and if you're short of money you should ask the school's secretary about getting free school meals.

Clothes will cost more as the child grows bigger and runs around more, so you should probably allow £3 a week. It is a good idea to set this aside so that when he needs an expensive pair of shoes or a winter coat the money is there to buy them. Older children demand more elaborate toys, like bicycles, but remember they will grow out of them or tire of them quite soon, so either buy second-hand or buy new and sell again later on. Use the library for books, except for birthday presents perhaps, and teach your children to use it: it will also save you money. As children get a bit older they often demand some pocket money for themselves. If you possibly can afford it, do give them a regular amount each week, even if it is not very much. It will be a great help in teaching them the value of money – so long as you don't let them have as much as they might like!

As children get older they often demand more pocket money.

From 11–16

Teenagers will eat more, their clothes cost more, hobbies and amusements cost more and school activities can cost a lot too. They are more likely to travel some distance to school by public transport, and they will ask for more pocket money. It could quite easily cost £1,000 a year if you sat down to add it all up. There is help to be had if you really need it and if your growing children want more than you can afford, try suggesting they earn a bit extra by cleaning cars or doing a paper round.

What help can you get?

Child benefit If you have children under nineteen who are still at school, ask at your social security office for a child benefit claim form. You need not have paid any NI and you will get £4·75 a week for each child. Remember that it is only if you qualify for child benefit that you will get the extra dependency allowance on most other benefits. If you are bringing up one or more children on your own, you will get an extra £3, called child benefit increase, for your oldest dependent child. However, you will not get the child benefit increase if you are getting a dependant's increase (except on an invalidity pension) or an allowance for the child at the higher rate of £7·50. If you are a lone parent and getting unemployment, sickness or maternity benefit you should take this child benefit increase rather than the extra 'dependant's addition' allowed for first children on top of unemployment, sickness or maternity benefit.

Family income supplement If you have any children and work for at least thirty hours a week (or twenty-four if you are on your own) and earn a low wage, you may get FIS. The amount depends on your income and how many children you have, but if you have one child and your earnings *before* deducting tax and NI are under £67 a week, you should claim. For each extra child the claim limit rises by £7 a week.

With 1 child and £40 a week you get £13·50, including £1 for heating.

With 2 children and £40 a week you get £17, including £1 for heating.

With 3 children and £30 a week you get the maximum for a three-child family of £20, including £1 for heating.

With 3 children and £50 a week you get £15·50, including £1 for heating.

Get a claim form from the social security or post office, and remember that you should not include child benefit or child benefit increase as part of your income.

Free milk and vitamins If you get FIS or Supp. B. you will get milk tokens and vitamins for all children under five. If you are married, with one child under five, and your income after rent or mortgage, rates, life insurance, fares to work, HP, and so on, is under £38, you might get these welfare benefits even if you don't get Supp. B. or FIS. If in doubt it will do no harm to try claiming – forms from social security or post offices.

Free glasses, prescriptions and dentist All children under sixteen get free health treatment, so always tell the chemist, optician or dentist how old the children are. Remember that you can get these free as well if you get FIS or Supp. B.; and even if you don't, it is always worth asking if your income is low.

Free school meals If you get FIS or Supp. B. your children will get free school meals, but you may qualify even if you don't get FIS or Supp. B., if you are a single parent or your income is low. Ask at the local education office at the town hall.

Additions to other benefits If you are getting any state social security benefits you should tell the social security that you have children. Then you may get some extra benefit. With retirement and widow's pensions, invalidity benefit and invalid care allowance you get an extra £7·50 a week for each child. With unemployment, sickness, and industrial injury benefit, and maternity allowance you get £1·25 unless you are over pension age, in which case you will get £7·50.

Supplementary benefit If you don't have a full-time job and can't make ends meet, see page 144 for whether you could get Supp. B.

Fares to school All school children can travel to school at half-price. Children under eight living more than two miles from the nearest school, and children over eight living more than three miles from the nearest school travel free. Ask at the local educational welfare office whose address you can get at the town hall.

Help with clothing Some local authorities may help with clothes and shoes needed for school. Ask at the local educational welfare office.

What if you are on your own?
It is bound to be harder, but you can get extra help:

Child benefit increase If you are divorced, separated or single you can get an extra £3 a week for your oldest child, but it is not worth claiming if you are on Supp. B. You need not have paid any NI. Ask at your social security office.

Child's special allowance If you are divorced and your ex-husband dies, you can get an extra £7·50 a week if he supported (or was supposed to support) the child before he died and paid NI. Again, ask for a form at your local social security office.

Educating children after they reach sixteen

If a child wants, or can be persuaded to get further qualifications at school, college, or through an apprenticeship, do everything you can to make it possible. His job chances will always be higher. Whenever they leave school, do make sure your children talk to the local authority careers officer before leaving. The school will probably arrange this, but talk to them yourself too.

If your child wants to go on to some sort of further training or education, you may be able to get help with the cost through central or local government schemes. Ask the careers officer or the school.

Children's own money

The sooner children learn to be responsible about money the better. Pocket money, and later an allowance, are a good way to learn, if you follow a few simple rules:

1 Always explain exactly what the money has to cover.
2 Never tell the child he is using his money in the wrong way; he'll find out soon enough when he runs out.
3 Try not to give a lot less than other children get – find out what they *really* get! Don't give a lot more either; it can result in begging by other children.

Children's savings   Many children like to save – for something in particular or just to hoard; encourage them. A piggy bank is fine to start with, but at seven or eight an NSB account of their own is a good idea; the post office is familiar, the accounts are easy to use, and they will get used to having a 'bank book'. At sixteen a current account at a High Street bank is a good idea, for either a wage or a college grant.

What to do when marriages go wrong

It is always unpleasant when marriages go wrong, but it will be a bit easier if the financial side of things can be sorted out as simply and cheaply as possible. You may need a solicitor if you want a divorce, especially if you have children, and solicitors can be expensive. However, you could run into even worse money problems if you don't get things properly arranged from the start. Remember that if you have been married for less than three years you can't get a divorce; a judicial separation, however, allows for a court order dividing the money and property.

The cost of getting a divorce

It could cost you £30 or so for an hour of a solicitor's time; so the more you can sort out between you before you call one in, the better. If you also need a barrister, which you will if there is to be a court hearing, you will have to pay for his time too. This may happen even where there is no argument at all. If there is any disagreement, it will cost far more.

Cutting your costs and getting help

1 Never think that because your husband or wife will be paying the bill the cost doesn't matter – there will be less for either of you if the bill if high.

2 Sort out as much as you can before calling in the professionals; they cost a lot.

3 If you have no children under eighteen and both want a divorce, you can get one by post without a solicitor. This only costs £20 or so, and if you have very little money, you can even apply to the court to waive this charge.

4 If you have children under eighteen, there will have to be a court hearing, with solicitors and barristers. Even so, if you have lived apart for two years and have no quarrel about either children or money, you can get a divorce costing hundreds rather than thousands of pounds.

5 You may be able to get help with legal costs through legal aid (see page 211). Under the Green Form Scheme, you are entitled to a couple of hours of a solicitor's time, either free of charge or at reduced cost, depending on your income. Even this short time will help with drafting the petition, registering a land charge on the home (see page 208) or applying for legal aid. You can ask for legal aid if there is to be a court hearing; you may be entitled to free or reduced cost advice, and it is always worth inquiring at a CAB or your solicitor first.

Maintenance

Usually the husband pays maintenance to his ex-wife, although it can be the other way round. Either way, you should try to arrange things so that there is as much money as possible for both of you – this is roughly what the court sets out to do. Try to agree the amount of maintenance and then get it agreed by the court so that the husband (or wife, if she is paying) can get tax relief on the payments. If there isn't a court order of this sort, the tax rules are such that the partner who is being maintained will end up with less (see page 30). A court order does not mean there is any reluctance to pay; it is just good sense from the money point of view. Remember that even if you are not getting divorced, a woman can apply to a court for a maintenance order if her husband fails to maintain her.

How much?   You will probably both have to make do with less than before, because there will be two homes to keep up; and there's no point in demanding more than your partner can afford. Normally, if a wife is not working she could expect to get about a third of her husband's income, plus a bit more for each child; however, many considerations will govern the court's decision on the amount. The court will aim to allow everyone, and in particular the children, to be as well off as before. The court will consider the incomes of both husband and wife, and their future earning power. It will also consider their ages, the ages of any children, and their other financial commitments. For example, if the wife could easily go out to work, she may get less. If the husband agrees to go on paying the household bills, he will not be asked to pay so much in maintenance.

If a wife is working she will get less, and maybe nothing at all; if the couple have not long been married and have no children, it is unlikely that either partner will have to pay maintenance. Remember that if a woman remarries, or lives with another man, her former husband will no longer be obliged to maintain her though he may still pay for any children.

Getting it paid With luck there will be no problem in actually getting your maintenance paid, but just in case:

1 If you think you won't get the money, ask the court to have the payments made through the Magistrates' Court. If the payments are not made, you can then apply to the court to enforce them.
2 Keep track of where your ex-husband lives and works.
3 If the money doesn't arrive, ask the court about getting an 'attachment of earnings'. This means that your payments will be taken straight off your husband's wages before he gets them.
4 If your husband gets a pay rise and you haven't got much to live on, ask the court to award you more. But if he loses his job he may ask to give you less.
5 If you want to get maintenance during the time your divorce is going through, you must apply on the divorce petition.

Dividing up the property
If you own your home It will almost always be the most valuable thing you own, and it can't be split down the middle. So what usually happens to it?

If you own it jointly, neither partner can sell without the other's agreement. The wife will usually be allowed to remain in the home if she is looking after the children. However, after school age, the house may have to be sold and the proceeds divided between the husband and wife.

If the husband owns the house, the wife should register her claim to stay there at the Land Registry in order to prevent her husband from selling the house before the court has reached a decision. Normally, when the divorce becomes absolute the wife will be allowed to remain in the home if she is looking after the children, and she may even be made the legal owner. The maintenance payments may include the mortgage repayments in which case the wife should check with the building society that these are being paid. Alternatively the wife may take on the mortgage, in which case, if her income is low, she may get help from social security or she can ask the building society to let her pay just the interest or to change to an option mortgage. The best thing is to talk to the building society.

If you rent your home   Again, it will usually be the wife who stays in the home if she is looking after any children. If the tenancy agreement was originally in the husband's name, the wife should ask for it to be transferred by the court to her name. She will then become responsible for keeping the home in good condition and for paying the rent and rates – although money for the rent may be included in her maintenance. If you are a council tenant, you should ask the council rather than the court, to transfer the tenancy to your name.

What about the bills?   When it comes to fuel bills, HP payments, and so on, whoever signed the agreement is responsible for paying the bills. If your husband signed but isn't paying, get in touch with the supplier and explain.

What if you weren't married?
If you have been living together for some time, you will be treated by the law in much the same way as if you had been married. However, a woman who lives with her partner but is not married to him would be wise to make sure she is joint owner of their house if she wants to be sure of being allowed to stay there in the event of a break-up.

Making your will

Many people don't like to think about making a will, but this is foolish for several reasons:

1 It's less miserable to make a will while you are healthy.
2 If you die without making a will, your relatives will have a muddle to sort out and will probably end up with less for themselves.
3 Unless you are very rich, your husband or wife will get everything if you don't make a will; so if you want anyone else to have anything at all you must make a will to say so.
4 If you have a lot to leave, making a will can mean there is less tax to pay, or the people you leave your property to will get more of it.

How to make a will
The simplest and cheapest way to make a will is to buy a 'will form' at a stationery shop. All you have to do is fill it in, and get two people to witness your signature – they need not see the will itself. This is only sufficient if your affairs are very simple, and even then you should get a book on making wills and make sure you know what you're doing first; it is surprisingly easy to put the wrong thing by mistake.

If your affairs are at all complicated, or you aren't sure about how to fill in the form, you will need a solicitor.

Decide exactly what you want to do with your property before you go to see one, and write it down; then you won't take so much of his time and the bill will be less.

Choosing an executor The executor sorts out your will and ensures that everything goes to the people you meant it to go to. He also arranges the funeral. You may want to choose a close relative, but it is a good idea to choose a professional as well – your bank or solicitor, for instance. They will charge for the service (perhaps £500 on property worth £10,000), but they know the ropes, and the money will be paid out of the estate after your death.

Changing your will If you get married you *have* to make a new will – any earlier one won't be valid. If you get divorced, have children or your husband or wife dies, you don't *have* to make a new will, but you may want to. It is always the most recent will that counts.

Challenging a will
If close relatives get nothing when someone dies, they can

ask the executors and a court to provide for them – if any property was left at all. A husband, wife, child (of any age), anyone treated as a child of the family or anyone who the deceased was maintaining prior to their death can make this claim; but if they are obviously capable of looking after themselves they are unlikely to succeed. If you want to make a claim, do it as soon as you can.

In Scotland the court will change a will that doesn't provide for these close members of the family, even if the family don't ask it to.

The cost of dying

Even the simplest funeral will cost £250 or more, and the death grant is only £30 or less (see page 158). The rest has to come out of what the deceased person leaves. However, if you are on Supp. B. or have a low income, and do not have a full-time job, and you have to arrange the funeral of a close relative, ask the social security office if they can help with the cost of the funeral. To keep the cost down you should get estimates from two or three firms if you can bring yourself to, and keep a check on the extras like notices in the papers or expensive out-of-season flowers.

Getting free legal help

Legal help is useful in all sorts of situations – an argument with a shop, a divorce, a row over a car accident, and so on. Unfortunately solicitors are expensive, but you can get help with the cost.

Legal advice If you get FIS or Supp. B., or have low earnings, you can probably get some legal advice for little or nothing. Go to a solicitor showing the legal aid sign and he should give you £25 worth of his time. This will only be an hour or two, or a couple of letters, but this should be enough to sort out a simple problem. Always get things as clear as you can in your own mind before you go to a solicitor, then you will get more done in the time.

To get this free legal advice ask at the CAB or the solicitor's office for a Legal Aid Green Form.

Legal Aid

Legal help in court If you get FIS or Supp. B. or have low earnings and few savings you may get help with a court case. This means you will get a solicitor to help you before the case and, if there is a court hearing, a barrister to appear in court for you. You will almost always get this sort of help if you are accused of a criminal offence, even if you have a reasonable income or savings.

To get free or assisted legal help for a court case, you should ask about 'legal aid' in a CAB or solicitor's office. If you have been accused of a crime and not allowed out on bail, ask a court official or prison officer as soon as you can.

Law centres If you live in a big city there may be a 'law centre'. These are staffed by solicitors and experienced

212

helpers, and are there to help you sort out any legal problem you may have. If the problem is simple you won't have to pay anything, and if you need more of a solicitor's time you will be told how to get legal aid.

Cabs and CACs Although they are not staffed by solicitors, both CABs and CACs will give you free help with simple legal problems and put you in touch with a solicitor if they think you need one.

13 Managing in retirement

After forty-five years or so of hard work you deserve a retirement that you can enjoy without money worries. There are three sorts of pension:

1 The state retirement pension.
2 A pension from your job.
3 A pension you buy for yourself by paying into a private pension fund.

By the time you retire it will be too late to start organizing a pension, or investing money to live on in your old age. So get things started as soon as you start work – a tiny bit put aside regularly for forty-five years will build up to a surprisingly large sum by the time you retire. When you get your first regular job, look at your pension prospects from all sources and decide if they look like being good enough; and remember to review the position every few years.

The state pension

Most people get a state retirement pension – men at sixty-five, women at sixty – provided they can be treated as being retired. The main groups of people who don't get one are women who have never worked, married women who have worked but who chose to pay the lower NI (see page 165) and people who have not paid enough NI.

What do you get?

Depending on the years you have worked an[...] will get a pension made up as follows:

1 **The basic pension**   This is £27·15 and £43·45 for m[...]ed couples where the wife does not have a pension of her own. To get it you must have been paying NI since you were sixteen, or since 1948 if you were already working then. If you have been ill or unemployed, your pension won't be affected so long as you registered at the time. However, if at any time you have not paid NI and *not* been registered as sick or unemployed, nor got exemption from paying, your pension will be lower, or you may get nothing at all. If you have stayed at home at any time since April 1978 to look after children or someone old or ill, you may have protected basic pension rights; ask at your social security office when you claim your pension.

2 **An earnings-related pension**   The size of this part of your pension depends on how much you earned after April 1978. The money may come from the state, or from your employer if he chose to opt out of the state scheme, but no 'contracted-out' employer's scheme can give you less than the state one would. Remember that you will not get any earnings-related pension if you have not worked for an employer and paid Class 1 NI – so the self-employed, for example, don't get it. If you have been ill or unemployed, the earnings-related part of your pension will be smaller, even if you registered at the time. If you earned £85 a week for twenty years till 1998, your earnings-related pension would be just over £15 a week, but if you retired in 1988, after paying into the scheme for only ten years, you would get about £7·50.

3 **Graduated pensions**   On top of your basic and earnings-related pension, you may be entitled to a graduated pension if you contributed to a scheme between 1961 and 1975. Married women who paid reduced rate NI, and do not get a basic or earnings-related pension may still be able to get a graduated one.

are a married woman   If you are working you will probably be paying full NI, so you will get an earnings-related pension and the basic pension of your own. If you have chosen to pay the lower rate of NI you may not get any pension of your own at all. Mrs K wrote to *Money-Go-Round* because she had worked all her life, paid the full NI contributions, and then discovered when she retired that she could have had a pension on her husband's contributions anyway. She said, 'I am the victim of a fraud, all those years paying in for a pension, and then not a penny.' The fact is, of course, that she and her husband would only have had £43·45 a week, instead of the two full pensions that they were getting, and she would have had to wait until her husband reached sixty-five and retired before getting her pension. This is the best reason for paying the full rate of NI (see page 166).

If you have never gone out to work, you will not have paid any NI, but you can still get a pension so long as your husband paid full NI. You will get £16·30 a week (so long as your husband has a full NI record and he is sixty-five), bringing your joint pension up to the married couple's rate of £43·45. If you stay at home for part of your married life and go out to work for part of it, you may earn some pension of your own. If you have been working and then stop to have a family, you will not lose the pension you have already earned. You can leave it where it is till you retire, add to it if you get another job later, and the years spent at home bringing up children may give you home responsibilities protection (see page 166).

If you are widowed   If your husband or wife dies after you are both retired, you can take over any pension he or she was getting, so long as it doesn't bring your total pension to more than the maximum for single people – your social security office will tell you if it does.

If you are already widowed when you reach retirement age, and you haven't married again, you can get a basic pension on your late husband or wife's NI.

216

If you go on working   If you have been accepted as retired, but then earn more than £52 a week during the five years after reaching retirement age, your pension will be reduced. If your earnings are high enough they may cancel out almost all the money you earn over the £52 limit, but after five years you can earn what you like without your pension being cut at all. In spite of the cut in your pension, it may still be worth going on working after you retire, and at least your earnings-related and graduated pension won't be cut at any time. If you do go on working, it will be better to put off drawing your pension at all for five years if you can, because by doing this you can earn extra pension for later. For example, if your pension would have been £20 a week at sixty-five, you could have £21·50 a week at sixty-six by going on working and not drawing it for a year. If you would earn enough to cut your pension by more than a couple of pounds a week, it will probably be worth giving it up altogether till you stop working. So if in any doubt, ask for leaflet NI92 at your social security office, which explains exactly how the sums work.

If you have been off work sick   You will still get a pension so long as you got exemption from NI. If you were getting invalidity benefit before retirement age you will, if you retire, get the retirement pension of £27·15, plus any additional and graduated pension, plus any invalidity allowance you were getting.

If you have a wife under sixty and children and get a retirement pension   You may get an extra £16·30 a week, so long as your wife doesn't earn over £45 herself. If she does, the £16·30 will be cut down, or stopped altogether. You will also get £7·50 for each child you still support.

If you change jobs   Changing your job can affect how your earnings-related pension is made up. If your last employer was in the state scheme and your next one is too, you needn't do anything – your pension will go on building up as before. If neither your last nor your next employer is in the state scheme, you may be able to take your pension with you – ask the personnel department or manager.

If you move from an employer in the scheme to one out of it, or the other way round, you still won't lose anything; when you retire part of your pension will come from the state and part from your employer. Always ask both employers what will happen to your pension before moving jobs.

If you are self-employed You will get the basic pension of £27·15, but no earnings-related addition. It is important to make your own arrangements for a better pension, because the basic one will not be enough on its own (see page 221).

If you are over eighty So long as you satisfy a simple residence condition you will get £16·30 a week, or more if you have paid enough NI contributions to earn any extra. Your wife may get £9·80 a week.

Age addition If you are over eighty you will get an extra 25p on your pension.

Claiming your pension

You will probably get a form from the social security about four months before you reach retirement age. If you don't, go and ask for one. If you are a married woman and will only be getting a pension on your husband's NI because you have never worked, you will have to claim when he reaches retirement age. If you are already sixty when your husband starts getting his pension you will probably be sent a form, but if you are not, go and ask for one. Remember that you should claim any graduated pension you may be entitled to yourself, when you retire.

Other help you may get
Supplementary pensions If you haven't got a full-time job and you have less than £27·15 a week to live on after paying the rent (or £43·45 for couples) you should ask about a supplementary pension. If you have special needs you might qualify if your income is a bit higher. There is no fixed rate, but generally your income will be made up to £27·15 a week (or £43·45 for couples) after rent. You don't have to have paid any NI to get this supplementary pension; just ask at your social security office.

Dental treatment and glasses If you get a supplementary pension these will be free; just tell your dentist or optician. If your income is low you may still get help to pay for them, even if you don't get a supplementary pension, so if in doubt ask at your social security office.

Free prescriptions Everyone over retirement age gets free medicines. Just fill in the form on the back of the prescription before you give it to the chemist.

Rent rebates If you get a supplementary pension it will already include an allowance for your rent. Otherwise, if you find it hard to pay the rent, ask your local authority about a rebate. Both private and council tenants can get them, and if you are a private tenant your landlord need never know.

A single person with an income of £40 a week and rent of £6 might get a rebate of £2. With a bigger rent or a smaller income you would get more.

Rate rebates If you get a supplementary pension your rates will already be included; otherwise, if you find it hard to pay the rates, ask your local authority about a rebate. You can get one if you own your home or if you are a tenant, so if you pay rent you should ask your landlord how much of it is for rates.

Local authority help Many local authorities organize meals on wheels, home helps, social clubs, reduced fares, residential homes, and so on. The sort of help available varies from one place to another, so if there is anything that would help you, ask at the local council social services department.

What if you're entitled to several benefits?

If you get a benefit such as industrial injury benefit, your basic retirement pension will be cut by that amount. So a single man getting industrial injury benefit of £23·40 would only get a basic pension of £3·75. However, supplementary pensions, and rent and rate rebates, are paid *on top of* your basic pension, and so is the attendance allowance for the severely disabled. Whatever benefits you get, the earnings-related part of your pension won't be cut down, and so a single person getting industrial injury benefit of £23·40 and an earnings-related retirement pension of £10 would get £37·15, made up of his injury benefit, his earnings-related pension, and the £3·75 left to him of his basic pension.

What if you go into hospital?

Your pension will not alter for eight weeks. Even after that you won't lose any of your earnings-related pension, but your basic pension will be cut to £16·25 – £38 if you have a dependent wife.

After a year in hospital you can have your pension paid to your wife (or any other dependant) and keep just £5·45 a week for yourself. Or you can have a bit less paid to your dependant and have some put aside for a resettlement benefit when you leave hospital. If you don't have any dependants your pension will anyway be cut to £5·45 a week, and you will be able to get resettlement benefit when you come out.

Do you need more than the state pension?
The basic pension of £27·15 (or £43·45 for couples) is hard
to live on. When the new state pension scheme has been
running for twenty years a couple could clock up a maximum
of nearly £100 a week including the full earnings-related
benefit, but many people would not get so much, and some
might need even more. You are likely to need more than the
state pension if:

- you are self-employed;
- you have been used to an income well above the
  maximum possible state pension;
- you are married and the wife has not paid full NI, so
  she has no pension of her own;
- you are a single woman and started work some years
  ago when you weren't allowed to join the company
  pension scheme; or
- you want to retire before reaching the state retirement
  age.

Ways of getting more money for your retirement
Pensions for the self-employed   You will need more than the
basic state pension, and the sooner you start putting money
aside the easier it will be. You are allowed to put 17½p in
every pound you earn into a private pension scheme, and
your contributions will get tax relief. If you earn a lot, this
tax relief will be worth a lot to you. You should get advice
from a life assurance company's pension department, your
bank manager or an accountant, because there are many
schemes available, one of which may suit you better than
another. Whichever you choose, you will not be able to get
your contributions back before the agreed retirement age,
so don't commit yourself to more than you can really afford.

Life assurance   Some with-profits endowment policies give
quite a good return (see page 132), and you will get tax relief
on the premiums. You can arrange things so that you get a

lump sum payment when you retire and you won't pay tax on it. Again, you should get expert advice before deciding which policy to go for, and if there is any chance that you will need to cash it in before you retire, ask about the penalties for doing so.

Annuities If you have invested in a life assurance policy, you may have quite a big lump sum when you retire; the same may be true if you get a golden handshake. A good way to turn this lump sum into the biggest possible income, is to buy an annuity with it. These are rather like instant pensions, and you buy them from life assurance companies. The drawback is that if you were to die quite soon after buying your annuity, all the money would stay with the life assurance company. To avoid this you should get either a 'joint life' or 'survivor' annuity, if you have a husband or wife who could benefit from the income after your death; or a 'guaranteed' annuity, which will go on paying the income to whoever inherits your estate, for an agreed period.

Earning a living Lots of people don't want to give up working completely when they reach retirement age. If you want to go on working remember:

- you should not pay any more NI, so get a certificate from the social security office and give it to your employer;
- if you earn more than £52 a week in the five years after retirement age, your basic state pension will be cut down, and you might do better not to draw it till you stop working (see page 217);
- so long as you fill in your tax form correctly (see page 25) you will not pay tax until you earn more than £35 a week – or £55 if you are married.

Useful addresses

If sending for leaflets from any of the following organizations it is always advisable to enclose a stamped addressed envelope.

Automobile Association
Offers a wide range of advice and services for members. Their head office is at Fanum House, Basingstoke, Hants, RG2 2EA.

British Insurance Association
Offers individual advice on various aspects of insurance except life assurance. Free leaflets available. Contact them at Aldermary House, Queen Street, London EC4 4JD.

Building Societies Association
Free information of a general sort on mortgages and investing in building societies. Contact them at 14 Park Street, London W1Y 4AL.

Consumers' Association
Publishers of *Which?* and its supplements. Unable to answer individual queries from non-members. Contact them at 14 Buckingham Street, London WC2.

Finance Houses Association
Offers general information on instalment credit. Contact them at 14 Queen Anne's Gate, London SW1H 9AG.

Life Offices Association
Offers an advisory service on life assurance. Free leaflets available. Contact them at Aldermary House, Queen Street, London EC4 4JD.

National Federation of Credit Unions
Lists addresses of credit unions. Their head office is at 11 Mead Close, Egham, Surrey, TW20 8JA.

National Federation of Self-Employed Ltd
Issues booklets and lists possible sources of funds. Contact them at 32 St Anne's Road West, Lytham St Anne's, Lancs, FY8 1NY.

Office of Fair Trading
Free leaflets on consumer credit, codes of practice and doorstep selling – all of which should be available in CABs. Contact them at Field House, 15-25 Bream's Buildings, London EC4 1PR *or* 9 Hope Street, Edinburgh EH2 4EL.

Royal Automobile Club
Offers a wide range of advice and services for members. Their head office is at 83-85 Pall Mall, London SW1Y 5HW.

Solid Fuel Advisory Service
Offers free advice on suitable fuels and heating systems. Contact them at Hobart House, Grosvenor Place, London SW1X 7AE.